Beyond the Harbour Lights

Chris Mills

Whittles Publishing

Typeset by
Whittles Publishing Services

Published by
Whittles Publishing,
Roseleigh House,
Latheronwheel,
Caithness, KW5 6DW,
Scotland, UK

www.whittlespublishing.com

ISBN 1-870325-64-8

Printed by Bell & Bain Ltd., Glasgow

Contents

Foreword vii

1   The Jungle Ship 1

2   A Mishap in Rangoon 7

3   The Last to Leave 13

4   Turning the Tables 19

5   Sudden Death in Buenaventura 25

6   Nous Maintaindrons 33

7   Call the Master! 38

8   A Master Censured 44

9   Mr Instone's Gold Medal 50

10   Roasted Maize 58

11   The Valuable Persian Carpets 62

12   Paradise on Earth 67

13   Hardship on Gardner Island 74

14   The Seventy-Third Time 80

15   Nearly on the Green 87

16   A Master's Salvage 92

17   A Strange Stowaway 97

18   Narrative of Operations 102

19	Running out of Coal	107
20	His Guardian Angel	113
21	Sailing Without Orders	119
22	A Heroic Second Mate	125
23	Mutiny on the S.S. *Luciston*	130
24	Admiralty Chart 1001	138
25	Making Legal History	144
26	The Confusing Harbour Lights	153

This book is dedicated to my daughter, Annette

NAME
MILLS

INCOME TAX CODE NUMBER AND DATE

S

15²/63

PENSION FUND AND REGISTERED No.

NATIONAL INSURANCE NUMBER
YH·48·09·11·C·

UNION OR SOCIETY
Name 855449 NUS
No.

GRADE NUMBER
AND DATE OF ISSUE OF CERTIFICATES OF COMPETENCY HELD

DECLARATION.

I DECLARE (i) that the person to whom this Discharge Book relates has satisfied me that he (she) is a seaman and (ii) that the photograph affixed bearing my official stamp is a true likeness of that person, that the signature within is his (her) true signature, that he (she) possesses the physical characteristics entered within and has stated to me the date and place of his (her) birth as entered within.

SIGNATURE OF SUPT. AT
MERCANTILE MARINE OFFICE

DATE

PHOTOGRAPH OF HOLDER

A782016
M.M.O. EMBOSSING STAMP

NAME OF SEAMAN.

*SURNAME (in Block Letters)
MILLS

*CHRISTIAN NAMES (in full)
CHRISTOPHER ALBERT

*Delete for Asiatics.

DATE AND PLACE OF BIRTH
22·1·1946· London

NATIONALITY
BRITISH

Height 5'8"
Eyes Blue
Colour of Hair Fair
Complexion Fair

Tattoo or other Distinguishing Marks
None.

Name, Relationship and Address of next-of-kin or nearest friend.

NAME Albert
RELATIONSHIP Father
ADDRESS 54, Hardwick Avenue, Croxley Green, Herts.

CHANGE IN ABOVE ADDRESS
3 CRAIGWELL AVE
AYLESBURY, BUCKS.

ADDRESS OF SEAMAN (if different from above)

CHANGE IN SEAMAN'S ADDRESS

B.S.C. Serial No. 78543 A

SIGNATURE OF SEAMAN
C. A. Mills

The author, aged 17, when he joined the Merchant Navy in 1963.

Foreword

Once British ships were to be found in every corner of the globe. Harbours around the world offered a safe haven to ocean-weary ships and in the majority of cases voyages made from harbour to harbour were uneventful. It was inevitable, with so many ships plying the world's trade routes, that sometimes an ordinary voyage could be turned into one full of drama and incident.

Newspapers generally had a shipping correspondent who provided a daily report of ships' movements, but if a ship entered harbour with news of an unusual voyage, the details were readily given space in the newspaper. In those days, shipping news was avidly read and reports often included photographs of ships in distress along with first-hand descriptions from those on board.

The author has supplemented a selection of contemporary newspaper articles with background information from other sources such as the reports of Marine Courts of Inquiry, extracts from ships' log books, and references to crew agreements, law reports and published narratives by ships' masters. A few imaginative details have been added, but the following stories are all firmly based on true events as reported and recorded at the time.

Chris Mills

Chapter 1

The Jungle Ship

The friendliest harbour light is a lightship anchored offshore which pin points the safe approach into harbour. The Boston Lightship stands out in Massachusetts Bay 10 miles from the harbour entrance. It is also the place where the pilot launch waits to rendezvous with incoming ocean freighters.

It was about 9 o'clock on the morning of 22nd April 1938 and the Boston pilot cutter lay in wait for the British Ellerman Line freighter S.S. *City of Salisbury*. The fog, patchy at first, was rapidly thickening and the Boston Harbour pilot, Captain William Lewis, was straining his ears to pick up some sounds from the approaching ship. At 9.45 am he was relieved to hear the deep, muffled blasts of a ship's foghorn and the cutter nosed forward to the meet the large ship as she ghosted in through the wisps of fog.

An hour later Captain Lewis was clambering up the dangling pilot ladder and was escorted up to the bridge by cadet Edgar Calvert. Captain Lewis had been a Boston Harbour pilot for twenty-five years and, as a senior pilot, felt confident he could bring any vessel into harbour with or without fog. The conditions had deteriorated and it was now rather doubtful if any of the harbour lights would help Captain Lewis get his bearings. Although he knew the waters of Boston Bay better than anybody, perhaps a pilot of lesser experience might have had second thoughts about taking the ship into harbour.

On a Thursday morning one month and twenty-two days before, in the sticky heat of Calcutta, Mehtab Singh Dua was overseeing the loading of crates of animals onto the decks of the *City of Salisbury*. He was a 38-year-old Indian who had built up a business supplying animals to American zoos, as well as a

1

steady trade in providing rhesus monkeys to New York medical schools. Mehtab had spent a long day supervising the loading of his latest consignment of animals, and was relieved when most of his crates were securely stacked on the relatively sheltered no. 3 hatch which was between the bridge deck and the funnel. There were twenty-two cages of colourful shama thrushes, eight boxes of cobras and pythons, sixteen large and strongly constructed crates each containing twenty monkeys. There was also a special crate for three small and rare Himalayan honey bears. In addition were many bags of food to keep the animals well-fed during the next two months.

The next day the *City of Salisbury* sailed for Rangoon, after which she called at Colombo and southern Indian ports before beginning the long voyage to Halifax. Her deep holds were crammed with 8,000 tons of exotic oriental produce – boxes of tea and spices, sacks of cashew nuts, rice, sugar and coconuts,

The City of Salisbury with a cargo of monkeys, bears, snakes and birds from India destined for American zoos ran aground and sank at the entrance to Boston Harbour. Photograph Leslie Jones 1938, courtesy of the Boston Public Library.

bolts of fine cotton, linen and silk, bundles of gunnies (coarse sacks) and hemp, bales of rubber and hides and jute, as well as more mundane goods such as pig iron and teak. The value of the cargo was in the region of US$1.5 million.

After almost two months of tending to the assorted daily needs of his animals, birds and snakes, Mehtab was looking forward to delivering them to their buyers. Feeding and cleaning the creatures had been a demanding job and whilst he had two assistants helping him, the success of the venture rested entirely on his shoulders. The three hundred monkeys demanded constant surveillance, a python had managed to escape and was rumoured to be amongst the coals in the ship's bunkers, and two cobras had been lost when one swallowed another and then died itself. A cold northern climate was not the best for his live cargo and he hoped that the ship would not spend too long at Halifax and Boston before going on to New York where his temporary zoo was to be delivered.

Captain Lewis entered the small wheelhouse of the *City of Salisbury* and shook hands with her master, Captain Owen Morris.

"Is this ship the Salisbury Zoo?" the American joked.

"Indeed we are, we'll be glad to see these animals ashore in New York," replied Captain Morris. "What do you think of this fog?" he added in a more serious note. In his own mind he felt that it would be prudent to anchor and sound the fog horn until visibility improved.

"It's a bit thick, Captain, but I think we can handle it." reassured the pilot.

Captain Morris glanced at the third mate, Robert Hull. They were both Welshmen and had sailed together on the *City of Salisbury* for the past few years and they were accustomed to the confidence and friendliness of the American pilots.

"You know , Captain, I do believe I've piloted this ship in before," drawled Captain Lewis and, turning to the third mate, he briskly ordered, "Half ahead, if you please."

The pilot had now assumed command of the vessel.

"What is your draught, Captain?" he asked, peering into the thick blanket of fog.

The ship's draught was 26 feet, and Captain Morris told him. Boston was a busy port and the Ellerman Line were regular callers. The *City of Salisbury* had been to Boston many times and it was quite probable that Captain Lewis had handled the ship before.

"OK, bring her round to N 45° W, and steady as she goes," snapped the pilot. The time was 11.09 am as the quartermaster repeated the order and eased the ship's wheel around until the compass needle settled on the course.

On the fo'c'sle head shrouded in cold clammy fog, Chief Officer Walter Owen was seeing that the towing and mooring lines were ready because in a short while a harbour tug would be on hand to help manoeuvre the ship into the inner harbour. He had also seen to it that the derricks of hatches 4 and 5 were topped and the tarpaulins over the hatches were loosened, so that the longshore men waiting on pier 2 could start unloading as soon as the ship docked. The carpenter, Leonard Duncan, stood by the windlass with his hand on the brake ready to send an anchor plunging at a moment's notice. The thick fog muffled all sounds and it was an eerie feeling to be standing at the bow of the ship moving through the grey swirling mist into Boston Bay, which was known to be a difficult pilotage.

Captain Lewis consulted his own Boston harbour chart. It was an extremely detailed chart compiled by the U.S. Coast and Geodetic Survey Department (Boston district) and its official reference number was chart 297. In fine weather Boston Bay was well-provided with navigation beacons and the pilots could navigate the ship in by sight, but, in fog, the chart was invaluable for it laid down set courses and distances that, when followed, would keep a ship well clear of any dangers. It was Captain Lewis' intention to steer N 45° W for half an hour, after which time he should either hear the whistle buoy on Shoals Spot Reef or, better still, spot the powerful flashing beam of the Graves Lighthouse. It was a proven method that he had used in thick fog before. The Graves Lighthouse was midway between the Boston Lightship and the harbour entrance; it was an essential aid to navigators since it marked the scattered dragon's teeth of rocks known as the Graves Ledges.

The soft ringing of the ship's bell marked 11.30 am and Captain Lewis, the collar of his overcoat turned up and his cap pulled down tightly on his head, stood far out on the port bridge wing straining his ears for the sound of the whistle buoy. He resolved to carry on for another five minutes before stopping the ship and listening for the distinctive signal that the buoy emitted. From the gloom of the fo'c'sle a metallic voice bellowed out of a megaphone.

"Breakers, breakers on the port bow!"

Captain Lewis reacted immediately, ordering full ahead and hard a starboard. The third mate forced the handle of the engine-room telegraph as far forward as it would go and the quartermaster spun the wheel hard over. It was too late. With a heart-stopping grinding that reverberated throughout the ship, the keel scraped along solid rock. Many bottom plates were ripped open and the ship jarred to a complete standstill. The engine was stopped and from somewhere ahead the faint but unmistakeable shriek of the whistle buoy became audible.

Without hesitation, Captain Morris resumed command of his sinking ship. Alarm bells rang, the lifeboats swung out and the crew donned their life-preservers. The carpenter was sent to sound the holds and peaks and the chief officer took soundings all around the ship. The *City of Salisbury* was taking water fast and began to settle and tilt over to starboard. Soundings indicated that the freighter was balanced on a ridge of rock amidships but had deep water under her bow and stern. Through infrequent clear patches in the fog, a bearing and distance from the Graves Lighthouse was taken and the ship's position was transmitted to Boston. A small flotilla of rescue craft scurried out to find the ship in the fog – five tugs, the Coastguard cutter, a pilot launch (for Captain Lewis) and the Harbour police boat all converged on the scene and by early afternoon the decision was made to partially abandon the ship. At 4.30 pm fifty-five lascar crewmen were taken off by one of the tugs, Captain Morris, his officers and Mehtab Singh choosing to remain on board. It would be a race against time to salvage the valuable cargo from the holds, but the immediate concern was to help the Indian entrepreneur save his animals and most of them were in fact taken off before the chill of nightfall.

The *City of Salisbury* had run aground at 11.39 am and incredibly, a few hours later, the story appeared in Boston's afternoon newspaper:

> 'ANIMAL-LADEN SHIP GROUNDS ON THE GRAVES
> The British freighter *City of Salisbury*, laden with snakes and ani-
> mals, inbound from Calcutta, ran aground on Graves Ledge 15
> miles off Boston in a heavy fog shortly before noon today and was
> leaking in all holds'.
>
> *Boston Traveller*, 22nd April 1938

The next day the Boston papers gave full coverage to what they nicknamed 'the jungle ship', their copy being enriched by many dramatic photographs, since it was not every day that a shipwreck occurred within the harbour limits.

The following day, Saturday, the morning sun melted the fog like magic, revealing the tall white Graves Lighthouse about a mile away, with even the hazy Boston shoreline visible in the distance. Chugging tugs put two lighters and a large floating crane at the stern of the ship and a tentative start was made by a gang of longshore workers to salvage some of the cargo. Mehtab Singh determinedly saw the very last box of snakes off the ship and, polite to the last, he sought out Captain Morris and thanked him for his help before hurrying to board a tugboat that was going into harbour. He had much to do, arranging customs clearance and alternative transportation for his zoo to New York.

It was midday when things took a turn for the worse. An ominous crack in the deck plating in front of the funnel appeared and everyone was promptly ordered to leave the ship by climbing into the motley collection of craft clustered around the stern. True to the tradition of the sea, Captain Morris was the last to leave the ship, clutching the ship's log book under his arm. Moments later the bow section broke off with an almighty roar, an event which was later summed up by Captain Owen Morris with a final entry in the log book:

> 'Steamer broke in half and fore part sunk with bridge deck above water and from stokehold aft also above water and steamer considered a total loss'.
>
> Official Log of the S.S. *City of Salisbury*, 23rd April 1938

For twenty-five years Captain William Lewis had been taking ships in and out of Boston, and was described as a 'harbour pilot veteran' by the local newspapers. In his report for the U.S. Bureau of Marine Inquiry which held an investigation into the shipwreck, he insisted that the rock the freighter had struck was not shown on chart 297, and that therefore he was not to blame. His confidence and instinct had tempted him to risk taking the *City of Salisbury* into a dense fog and that is how the 'jungle ship' came to grief on Boston's doorstep.

Chapter 2

A Mishap in Rangoon

High on a hill, the great golden dome of the Shwe Dagon Pagoda has long dominated Rangoon. The city lies on the north bank of the fast-flowing Rangoon River and in its heyday rivalled Calcutta and Bombay as a great eastern port. One of the busiest streets was the long and straight Monkey Point Road which ran along the waterfront. On one side were the wharves and warehouses and on the other the crowded and colourful open fronted shops and main buildings of the city. There were no docks in Rangoon, ships tied up along the river's waterfront or at busy times moored to buoys in midstream. Sailors going ashore knew Monkey Point Road very well for it had many attractions such as the Seamens' Institute, numerous bars, Chinese tailors, Indian money changers and Burmese cheroot merchants.

In October 1918 the Great War was drawing to a close, the talk of an armistice was gathering momentum and the British Government was able to release some merchant ships from Army supply transport duties and return them to regular trading. The Henderson Line of Glasgow was able to place one of its fleet, the S.S. *Tenasserim*, back into its Glasgow–Liverpool–Suez–Rangoon service. The company had pioneered this direct service from the UK to Burma in the 1870s and competition by officers for a berth on one of the 'Burma boats' was intense. The *Tenasserim* (named after the Burmese district of that name) had been built especially for the Henderson Line in 1905, her four spacious holds being designed to enable valuable trunks of teak and mahogany to be stowed more easily. Another feature of the holds was that they were well ventilated which was essential for the carriage of bagged rice – exotic timbers and fine rice being Burma's main exports. The ship also had superb first-class accommodation for passengers, with the cabins, saloon and the smoke-room being lined with luxurious polished teak woodwork.

Captain C. Plage, aged 40 and a native of Glasgow, was the master of the *Tenasserim*. On 17th October 1918 at the Mercantile Marine Office in Glasgow, he attended the signing-on of thirty-two Scottish officers (the 60 crew were signed-on under 'Lascar Articles', British ships regularly trading to India and Burma carried Indian crews) and noted that a new chief engineer, John Brown, was coming on board. A few months previously, a wartime Government directive had earmarked the *Tenasserim* for conversion from coal to oil as fuel. Captain Plage imagined that this innovation would now no longer be necessary and he and his officers looked forward to leaving a freezing cold Scotland behind them and enjoying their first peace-time voyage for many a year. They were to be disappointed, for 'red-tape' would not allow the ship to commence her voyage until the conversion work had been done. However, Chief Engineer John Brown looked on the bright side as he for one appreciated the opportunity to gain some first-hand experience with the use of oil. It was something that was, in fact, new to all the ship's engineers and none had received any training in firing ships' boilers with oil instead of coal. In theory, the idea of using the ship's water ballast tanks for the storage of the thick black oil was sound, but converting these tanks, some of which were situated beneath the boilers, caused some misgivings. Their concerns were lessened when they learnt that, along with the conversion, came a modern fire extinguishing system of steam-smothering apparatus.

The conversion work was speedily completed by the yards at Birkenhead and, to the relief of all, once tested and passed by the Board of Trade Surveyors, the *Tenasserim* was given clearance to load and to sail. The newly adapted oil storage tanks beneath the boilers would be filled at Suez and until then the boilers would be using coal from the ship's bunkers. On the very eve of departure, Chief Officer Reid was busy supervising the loading of a consignment of high explosive shells and boxes of rifle cartridges for the 1–70th Burma Rifles. This dangerous cargo was secured in a special compartment with only the chief officer having the key. Steam was raised and as the vessel eased out into the Mersey, the third engineer was suddenly taken ill and sent to hospital. Unable to replace him at such short notice, the *Tenasserim* was cleared to sail and she left Liverpool on 2nd November 1918.

In the engine-room, Fourth Engineer Andrew Potter was promoted to Third, and Fifth Engineer George Scotland was promoted to Fourth. They were both uncertificated junior engineers but had sailed in the ship before and knew the engine-room well. Sailing shorthanded was not unusual due to the War.

A few days later, another unexpected promotion took place when the senior wireless officer and the surgeon showed symptoms of the dreaded Spanish 'flu. Captain Plage hurriedly took the *Tenasserim* into Gibraltar to land the sick men and to have their cabins fumigated. There was no replacement for the surgeon, but Assistant Wireless Operator William Haughey, an 18-year-old lad from Greenock, found himself in sole charge of the ship's wireless equipment, his wages increasing from £4.10s a month to £7 (plus £3 war risks bonus). His first important duty was to joyfully inform Captain Plage that the armistice had been signed. It was an event which had been anticipated and from then on the officers continually pressed the young Sparks for news from home.

Passing through the Suez Canal and taking on oil fuel at Port Tewfik, the ship made the switch from burning coal to oil. A routine call was made at Colombo on 7th December, and after a smooth crossing of the Bay of Bengal it wasn't too long before the spotless white Rangoon pilot boat was sighted on station south of Elephant Point. It was then a tricky 20-mile pilotage up the Rangoon River, but for the crew it was the intoxicating earthy smells of mangroves, steamy jungle and endless fields of rice that marked the end of the ocean passage. On the bridge the pilot and his assistant took little notice of the scenery, but were intent on taking bearings of the golden dome of the Shwe Dagon Pagoda, which was very handy for checking the ship's progress. The *Tenasserim* was expertly berthed at the Henderson Line's wharf opposite Sule Pagoda Road. The strength of the tides and currents of the great river meant that ships lying at the wharves had, besides their ordinary mooring lines, heavy chains made fast fore and aft. The river had its moods and all craft from ocean-going steamers to the ubiquitous sampans needed to be constantly on guard against its dangers.

Rangoon was a vibrant city and the waterfront was a shambles of warehouses crammed with sawn timber, sacks of rice, spices, tobacco, silks and other tropical produce. The day started early as most business was done in the cool of the morning, but by afternoon the heat was unbearable. It was mid-afternoon before a hot and bothered Captain Plage had time to gaze down on the crowds of Indians, Chinese and Burmese labourers who worked on the waterfront. He knew the city well having been there many times before and, as he watched the mixture of humanity below him, he spotted a procession of saffron-robed Buddhist monks. Suddenly he distinguished a figure dressed in a white linen suit and wearing a white solar topee – he smiled as he recognized an old friend, Mr Goldsmith, the Henderson Line's agent in Rangoon. A perspiring Mr Goldsmith came on board and was greeted warmly by Captain Plage. Part of the ship's business was that there were over sixty European passengers eagerly waiting to come on board and since the *Tenasserim* was the only ship to be sailing directly to to the UK in the forseeable future, cabin space was at a premium. Anxious to turn the ship around quickly, Mr Goldsmith had arranged for the steamer to move across the river to the Burmah Oil Company's bunkering mooring at Syriam, where cargo work would continue using lighters.

A few days later, on 18th December, the *Tenasserim* left the wharf and slowly moved downriver – past Monkey Point and across the wide mouth of the Pegu River to Syriam, a distance of about 4 miles. It was evening before the ship was securely chained fore and aft to the mooring buoys opposite the Burmah Oil Company's oil storage tanks and preparations to take on 650 tons of oil began immediately. Chief Engineer John Brown and Fourth Engineer Scotland supervised the oiling. One of the double bottom tanks, No. 4, was still full of Port Tewfik oil, and it was decided to fill the remaining three tanks in the order Nos. 2, 3 and 1. Experience at Port Tewfik had shown that no matter how much care was used, overflows were difficult to avoid and Chief Engineer Brown was mindful of the fact that No. 2 tank was directly beneath the starboard boiler (which remained fired-up at an inside temperature of 365°F). He spent several tense hours checking and rechecking the hose connection for leaks or overflows until by midnight he declared that No. 2 tank was full. The two engineers then concentrated on filling the other two tanks and by 5 am the job was complete and Chief Engineer Brown retired to his cabin, leaving the Fourth Engineer to tidy up.

Left down below, George Scotland put the engine-room crew to work in preparation for handing over the watch at 6 am. At ten minutes to six, two of the Indian firemen shouted that there was a fire under the starboard boiler. George Scotland anxiously hurried into the stokehold to take a look and, to his consternation, he saw that a fierce fire had indeed broken out. He raced up the steep engine-room ladders and burst into the chief engineer's cabin, breathlessly gasping out that the engine-room was on fire. Chief Engineer Brown demanded to know if the steam smothering apparatus had been opened up, but the young Fourth Engineer had to admit that it had not. Raising the alarm, the two men hurtled down the ladders into the bowels of the engine-room and turned on the steam jets that were supposed to smother any fire. Choking black smoke and red flames seemed to be everywhere and the thick blanket of released steam had little effect. It was obvious that the engine-room was not steam tight and that steam alone could not dampen the fire down. Chief Engineer Brown then made the frightening discovery that it was the oil in no. 2 double bottom tank that was on fire! The fact that this tank was situated beneath the stokehold deck plating made it impossible to reach with chemical extinguishers or buckets of sand. By this time, Captain Plage had put the entire crew at fire-fighting stations, and all the ship's firehoses were directed down into the engine-room in an effort to cool the red-hot steel decking. At first this seemed to beat the flames down but, unaffected by water, the oil-fed flames roared up fiercer than ever and a plume of greasy smoke rose up out of the engine-room skylight.

By 7am the fireboats *Water Lily* (Burmah Oil) and *Firefly* (Irrawaddy Flotilla) were alongside, but their powerful hoses had no effect on the blaze. In fact the water was simply spreading the burning oil into every nook and cranny of the engine-room, and when a series of explosions turned everything into a fiery cauldron, Captain Plage gave the order to abandon ship. The crew tumbled over the side of the steamer onto the fireboats, Chief Officer Reid and Captain Plage being the last to go. Shortly afterwards of his own volition, Chief Officer Reid led a small group of port officals back on board in an attempt to dump the live ammunition belonging to the Burma Rifles overboard. Captain Plage also returned with Principal Port Officer Captain Hordern to assess the prospects of saving the *Tenasserim*. Finding that the fire was completely out of control, they concluded that nothing could be done and that the ship was doomed, so for a second time the order was given for everyone to get clear of the burning ship.

In Rangoon, people took up vantage points to view the rising column of smoke issuing from the Henderson Line steamer, and under the blaze of the midday sun the bedraggled and soot-blackened crew was landed at Sparks Jetty. Under the curious gaze of many onlookers, they made the short walk to the Mayo Seaman's Institute on Monkey Point Road. There was a rumour that the *Tenasserim* had been sabotaged by German agents, but Chief Engineer Brown knew better than that. With the recent end of the war and the advent of Christmas and Hogmanay, it was the festive season in Rangoon. However, the sight of a proud British steamer burning day after day made a sad backdrop to the festive season. A bright New Year dawned and on 8th January 1919 a Court of Marine Inquiry into the cause of the fire was held at Rangoon Magistrates Court. The Court found it likely that fuel oil from no. 2 double bottom tank had either leaked or overflowed and had spread under the starboard boiler, where it had become heated causing it to ignite. This conclusion could not be verified because the ship was still a mass of flames, which showed no signs of abating after twenty days.

> 'It seems unlikely that the ship will be saved from complete
> destruction as the fire is still burning furiously'.
> Court of Inquiry, Rangoon, 8th January 1919

Other findings were that no-one was directly to blame and no engineers' certificates should be cancelled or suspended. The loss of the *Tenasserim* had been a mishap and it was a sad end for a merchant ship that had successfully dodged U-boats for the past four years. The Court also recommended improvements, such as the fitting of pressure gauges to warn of any overflow of oil, so that an engine-room could be effectively sealed in the event of a fire.

The following week the *Tenasserim* made a dramatic farewell when, still blazing from stem to stern, she heeled over and sank. The wreck is marked on the Rangoon chart and lies in the deep water between Hastings Shoal and the Syriam Signal Station. The days passed slowly as Captain Plage and his officers waited patiently for a ship to take them home. Eventually after four months they had all gone, leaving just the captain behind. He had been in Rangoon so long that he had grown accustomed to life ashore – the call of the temple bells, the daily ritual of tiffin, or relaxing in wicker chairs sipping sundowners.

Many years later, at his home on University Avenue, Glasgow, Captain Plage often recalled those four months ashore in Rangoon. He knew the city's roads as well as Argyle and Sauchiehall Streets and sometimes, when the cold winter winds swept over Glasgow, he remembered Monkey Point Road together with the words of Rudyard Kipling:

> *For the temple bells are callin',*
> *an' it's there that I would be ...*

Chapter 3

The Last to Leave

Christmas Day in the South Seas was a time of festivity. In Suva, Christmas Eve passed merrily with many of the European merchants and planters gathering together in their clubs, whilst in the streets crowds of native Fijians and Indians thronged the shops and bars. Christmas Day saw things quieten down and the police were able to report that Suva, as a whole, was most orderly. However 500 miles to the east in Vavau's harbour, the S.S. *Clan MacWilliam* was blazing furiously and celebrating Christmas Day was the last thing on anyone's mind.

> 'In the little land-locked harbour of Vavau on Christmas Day 1927, the good ship *Clan MacWilliam* lay. In some manner, at present unknown, her cargo of copra had caught fire and was blazing furiously. Presently the ship's powers of resistance came to an end and, buckling up, she sank. She became a total loss. But for the existence of insurance companies, Christmas Day 1927 would have been a Black Christmas indeed for many a planter and many a merchant in Fiji'.
>
> *The Fiji Times & Herald*, 3rd January 1928

On 23rd July 1927 the Clan Line steamer *Clan MacWilliam* sailed from her home port of Glasgow. The ship's complement of fifteen white officers and sixty-one Indian crew expected to be away for at least a year for the ship's ports of call were not known for certain. Clan Line vessels, with their black funnels with twin red bands, were easily recognized, particularly east of Suez, and round-the-world voyages via the South Pacific were commonplace. The large fleet of

Scottish freighters was well-maintained and the Clan Line was thought of as being a good company by those who sailed with them. In particular, elderly Chief Engineer Dishington, who had spent his entire working life in the engine-rooms of Clan Line ships, had arrived at the strange conclusion that he was destined to die on board the *Clan MacWilliam*. The Clan Line was known as the 'Scots Navy' as it had a large fleet and the officers wore a uniform similar to the Royal Navy, in that the gold rings of rank on the sleeves had a loop and not the traditional diamond of the Merchant service.

After calling at Birkenhead and Newport, the ship began her long voyage in earnest. Initially the weather was temperate but, as the ship travelled further east, the fierce Arabian sun beat down on the decks and the ship became hotter than an oven, in spite of the canvas awnings that were rigged. The officers changed into their whites, which included the pith helmet if they wished. Passing through Suez and the Red Sea, Durban was eventually reached, by which time all outward cargo had been cleared. Bunkers and fresh water were taken on and the fuel oil in her forward double bottom tanks was topped up. The boilers could be fired by coal or oil giving the ship enough fuel to go far off the beaten track. Exports of coal had made Durban a prosperous port and the ship was loaded with 7,000 tons of coal for Batavia in the Dutch East Indies. The *Clan MacWilliam* plodded her way across the Indian Ocean and, after discharging at Batavia, she proceeded in ballast into the South Seas. Her orders were to call at New Caledonia, Fiji, Tonga and Samoa to fill her holds with chrome ore, timber and copra before returning home via the Panama Canal. A voyage on any of the Clan Line steamers would take a seaman to the most beautiful and out-of-the-way places on the globe.

Leaving Batavia, Captain William Thomson, master of the *Clan MacWilliam*, carefully took his ship through the scattered reefs and islands of the Arafura and Coral Seas to the next port of Noumea. After filling the lower holds with heavy chrome ore, two days of glorious steaming saw the ship approaching Viti Levu, the main island of Fiji, entering Suva harbour on 7th December,

Suva, the 'Queen of South Sea ports', was a colourful scene of activity as steamers from Europe, Australia, New Zealand and the United States called regularly, and it was a port of call for Clan Line vessels. In addition to the procession of ocean steamers, the harbour was alive with small inter-island craft loaded to the gunwales with people and produce. Fronting the harbour were the solid white buildings containing the seat of the Crown Colony's administration, as well as the offices of the many British and Australian companies serving the South Pacific. To the Scots on board the *Clan MacWilliam*, the vivid emerald scenery, the heat, sights and sounds of Fiji made such an impression that celebrating Hogmanay would be rather special that year. In Suva, Christmas was an important time and that year cards with views of the island were popular, many being sent back to the old country. The Coconut Planters' Union routinely exported copra to Europe and a mountain of bulging sacks of the sun-dried coconut kernels had been stockpiled awaiting the Clan Line steamer's arrival.

Stowage of cargo is the responsibility of the chief officer and Murray Maclean had supervised the loading of copra many times before; he was used to the rank, oily stink of dried coconut pervading the ship. Copra has an oil content of 66% and the danger of fire is ever present. In the United Kingdom, the extracted coconut oil was an expensive commodity and was used in the manufacture of margarine and soap. The large jute sacks filled with the dried coconut were stowed on top of the chrome ore and ensuring good ventilation became the preoccupation of Chief Officer Maclean. If the weather was good it was common practice at sea to take the hatch boards off at each end of the holds to allow clean air to flow through to keep the copra fresh, as well as clearing out dangerous fumes. In the ship's deep holds the copra was liable to overheat and the fear of fire was constant. The jute sacks became impregnated with oil and, together with the rich oily copra, created a closely packed mass of extremely flammable material.

After loading 1,319 tons of copra and 500 feet of rare Kauri timber, the ship left Suva and coasted around to Levuka, before leaving Fijian waters and going to the islands of Tonga and Samoa. The loading ports were Nukualofa, Vavau and Apia, where further copra was waiting. Once loading was completed at Nukualofa, the *Clan MacWilliam* steered northward for the small island of Vavau where it seemed likely that the ship would spend Christmas, with New Year's Eve at Apia. The Clan Line had been sending vessels into the South Seas for a long time and their captains were advised to follow the set courses (weather permitting) as recommended by the company. Being heavily loaded with 3,000 tons of chrome ore and 3,000 tons of copra, even the most experienced master was never at ease taking his ship through the reef-studded South Seas.

Speed was reduced in order to arrive off Vavau Island in the early morning as it was too dangerous to enter the harbour of Neiafu at night. By first light of 23rd December 1927, Vavau's unmistakeable steep cliffs and remarkable flat-topped Moungalafa Hill made an imposing sight. Speed was eased further as a battered pilot launch ventured out to meet the ship. Neiafu is one of the most sheltered harbours of the Pacific Islands and is entered by means of a narrow twisting channel. Only the local pilot has the knowledge of the tides and currents and the leading marks and coloured buoys to take a large ship into harbour. By 7.30 am the *Clan MacWilliam* was safely tied up at the small wooden wharf, the stillness of the morning being broken by the clanking of winches as the derricks were topped and the two foredeck hatches opened to receive several hundred tons of copra.

Labour gangs of islanders stood waiting and soon the foredeck was a hive of activity as sling after sling of bulging sacks of copra were swung on board. Loading continued throughout the day, but the energy of the islanders slowly waned and they gradually adopted a slower pace. The officers of the ship were looking forward to Christmas Day which was, of course, a holiday on the island, and most of them planned to visit the church which overlooked the harbour. During Saturday, 24th December the islanders toiled away at stowing the awkward sacks and it was decided to pay them overtime to work on into the night to complete the loading. Being Christmas Eve, the officers congregated in the saloon, although they couldn't relax completely as the ship was still working cargo. At midnight it was Second Mate Joseph Mellor's turn to take the watch on deck, and he went onto the foredeck with Apprentice Freestone to relieve Third Mate Woolfauden who was standing at no. 2 hatch. First Mate Maclean and Fourth Mate Watkins also decided to a take a stroll on deck to get a breath of fresh air. The four deck officers and the young apprentice stood together watching the islanders sweating and straining under the clusters of deck lights to force the weighty sacks into the hold. The chief officer advised the second mate to continue for another hour before calling a halt and then to transfer the labourers to no. 1 hold.

It was pleasant enough out on deck, the night was warm and it had been a long day. The other officers left Second Mate Mellor and the apprentice to their duties and turned in. Obeying the chief officer's instructions, the second mate waited an hour before calling a halt to the loading and the labour gang shuffled without haste to the adjoining no. 1 hatch. At about 2 am, Aleck Williams, a Samoan foreman, went back to no. 2 hold suspecting that some of his men were sleeping in there. He stiffened and gave a loud yell as he caught sight of a dull flickering of flame amongst the top layer of recently-stowed sacks. Hearing the commotion, the second mate and the apprentice hurried along the cluttered deck to see what it was all about. They saw the fire immediately and Apprentice Freestone was told to get up to the fo'c's'le head and ring the ship's bell for all he was worth. The harsh clanging sounded the alarm and as Captain Thomson and his officers appeared, the panic-stricken natives scrambled down the gangway and onto the wharf.

Captain Thomson quickly took charge and had the crew run out the fire hoses to fight the fire. Everyone on board optimistically believed that by thoroughly soaking the area around the sacks, the fire could be controlled. However, the gushing sea water had little effect and the vivid red tongues of flame began to roar and spit in the darkness. There was fuel oil in the double bottom tanks beneath no. 2 hold and Captain Thomson ordered the hold to be flooded. The harbour master, grasping the awful reality of what was happening, directed Captain Thomson to cast off from the wharf and anchor the ship in deep water. This was done and the ship's lifeboats were swung out and lowered in readiness for abandoning ship. The hold was completely waterlogged making the vessel sink low in the water but the fire was still spreading. No. 1 hold was flooded, with Captain Thomson declaring, "We'll take the old ship home yet!"

The intense heat generated by the inferno radiated through the steel bulkheads and caused the varnished woodwork on the bridge to erupt into flames, and then no. 3 hold directly behind the bridge began to burn. The entire population of Neiafu ringed the harbour to view the burning ship which lit up the night like a huge beacon. As the hours passed, the foremast toppled over and the sides of the ship buckled and caved in and by morning the *Clan MacWilliam* was a sorry sight. Spirals of smoke swirled up hundreds of feet in the air and the spectators willed the crew to leave the cauldron of heat and smoke and save their lives. However, in spite of everything, the crew stubbornly fought the flames in the belief that even if the ship's decks were awash, she would not sink in the calm waters of the harbour and the fires would be drowned. They were wrong, for the oil-rich copra continued to burn at furnace strength, and, accepting the inevitable, Captain Thomson gave the order "All hands take to your boats! Lose no time in getting away! No. 1 boat, you stand by!"

The crew, with the exception of Chief Engineer Dishington, needed no encouragement and hurried into the waiting lifeboats. Second Mate Mellor, who was in charge of no. 1 lifeboat, glanced upward and wondered where Captain Thomson and Chief Engineer Dishington were and why they had not taken their places in his lifeboat. He was in a terrible dilemma. He could not cast off and leave the two men behind, but with the fire roaring and crackling it was certain that something disastrous was about to happen. There was no sign of the two missing men. Suddenly, an ear-splitting boom blasted the ship apart. The midships section of the steel hull crumpled like cardboard and the stem and stern rose violently into the air and almost touched. The whole ship plunged underwater with an almighty hiss as a series of underwater explosions made the sea bubble and boil. By pure good fortune, although deluged by water and showered with flying debris, the lifeboat survived the explosion and slowly pulled to shore. Captain Thomson and Chief Engineer Dishington were never seen again. Captain Thomson would not leave whilst the chief engineer was still on board, a stand-off which resulted in the two men going down with the ship.

Bad news travelled fast, and it was only two days later when the first account of the tragedy appeared.

'STEAMER LOST
CLAN MacWILLIAM CAPTAIN AND ENGINEER DROWNED

We regret to report that the S.S. *Clan MacWilliam* caught fire whilst loading copra in Vavau. The first messages received from the agents in Tonga, Morris Hedstrom Limited, reported that holds 1 and 2 were on fire, but that it was hoped to control the fire. Later messages sent on Saturday night stated that the fire had spread to no. 3 hold and that a total loss was feared.

... We learn her cargo was fully covered by insurance with the Liverpool & London & Globe Insurance Co. Limited and other companies. The agents of the L & L & G state that they wrote policies on the cargo by the vessel amounting to just under £30,000'.

The Fiji Times & Herald, 28th December 1927.

Chapter 4

Turning the Tables

T he S.S. *Sunning* was a medium-sized passenger steamer, built in Hong
Kong in 1916 specifically to trade between the Crown Colony and
Shanghai. Although her port of registry was London, the vessel never
actually left Chinese waters as all her surveys for seaworthiness were done in the
British territory of Hong Kong. The *Sunning* was one of a fleet of ships and
riverboats owned by the China Navigation Company. The company offered an
attractive career to British Merchant Navy officers who wished to have exciting,
secure employment in the Far East. There was only one drawback – the Chinese
coast was alive with ruthless pirates.

'Chinese Pirates
The sensational fiction of the sea has nothing more thrilling to offer than
the story of the *Sunning* piracy. Here are all the ingredients for the most
lurid of nautical yarns – officers over-powered by Chinese pirates who
had come aboard as passengers; the bridge recaptured by two officers
who felled the pirates to the deck with blows from a leaden weight; the
other officers released and a three-hour fight with the pirates in which
eleven are shot down and roll over the unprotected side of the ship to
meet their fate in the sea; the one lady passenger sent off in a ship's boat
for safety and rescued later by a British warship; the ship set fire to by the
pirates but saved by the seamanship of the Captain; ultimately nearly all
the pirates rounded up and brought to justice and the disabled vessel towed
into port'.

The Straits Times, 20th November 1926

Casting off from the China Navigation Company's wharf at Shanghai, 53-year-old Captain James Pringle, master of the *Sunning,* gave a sigh of relief. The expected consignment of gold bullion had been cancelled and, with piracy being so rampant, he was relieved not to have such a cargo onboard. The ship was manned by a Chinese crew of sixty-five and in Shanghai it was impossible to keep any shipment of a valuable cargo secret. As well as carrying several thousand tons of general goods for Hong Kong, the *Sunning* would as usual be carrying a considerable number of passengers. Seventy Chinese packed the deck space, whilst a Russian woman and a European man each had a first-class cabin. In addition another eighty Chinese deck passengers were to be picked up at Amoy further down the coast.

The S.S Sunning *before the pirates boarded her.*

Captain Pringle, an old China hand, had been in and out of Shanghai countless times but it was never easy taking a ship out into the estuary of the Yangtze which was always congested with junks, sampans, lighters and rusty steamers, many of which did not follow any recognizable 'rules'. Like most China Navigation Company officers, Captain Pringle felt more at home in Hong Kong where the company had established its headquarters more than fifty years before. The China Station of the Royal Navy had also been long-established at Hong Kong and in 1926 their presence was very much needed. Piracy had become a major concern for all merchant shipping and China itself was in turmoil as a series of civil wars raged across the country.

Armed anti-piracy guards were being employed on many large ships plying the Chinese coast and the *Sunning* carried four guards supplied by the Royal Hong Kong police and, in common with other company vessels, access to her bridge was restricted by iron grilles and gates which were kept locked at sea. The *Sunning* had been ransacked by pirates three years previously and Captain Pringle knew from experience that the pirate gangs did not hesitate to kill anyone who got in their way. It had even become company policy to issue firearms to all officers who, along with their naval-type uniforms, had the appearance of being part of the Royal Navy.

Leaving behind the intrigue and unrest of Shanghai on Saturday, 13th November 1926, the *Sunning,* whose four holds were brimming with cargo and her decks occupied by Chinese passengers, picked her way through the jumble of native craft and out into the open sea. Her six British officers looked forward to a peaceful week's voyage to Hong Kong with just one call at Amoy. Only the prospect of running the gauntlet of the notorious pirate haunt of Bias Bay, 50 miles north of Hong Kong, spoilt the prospect of what was otherwise a pleasant sea trip. Once at sea, the officers settled down to the routine of standing watches four hours on and four hours off, with the captain and the chief engineer being almost constantly on duty. Second Mate John Hurst and Second Engineer William Orr were both newcomers to the company and had been attracted by the prospect of adventure and the good pay and conditions. They each owned an identical pearl-handled Colt revolver, which they always carried with them when they went ashore in the lawless Chinese ports.

After four days at sea, the *Sunning* touched at Amoy to take on eighty or so deck passengers. They crowded on board and were herded aft by the comprador (a Chinese contractor in charge of deck space and catering) and his 'teaboys' – young, tough assistants). Within the hour, the ship was again on her way towards Hong Kong. About the same time, 200 miles to the south, HMS *Bluebell* signalled to the *Sunning* that she was on patrol and would escort the merchant ship across the dangerous waters of Bias Bay. In the dining saloon that evening, Captain Pringle was able to pass on the good news to the first class passengers – Madame Prokieva, the Russian lady and Mr. Lapsley, a European who was fluent in several Chinese dialects.

His evening meal over, Second Officer Hurst went up to the bridge to relieve Chief Officer Beatty for the 6 to 8 dog watch. Night was coming on and he made sure that the ship's steaming lights were burning brightly. The large junks that plied the coast rarely displayed lights, but relied on other vessels' lights to avoid collision. He was peering forward when somebody grabbed his legs and pulled him to the deck! Two shadowy figures then forced him at gun-point to get up and lead them down the companion ladder leading to the deck below and into Captain Pringle's cabin. On being confronted, Captain Pringle immediately surrendered because he knew that any attempt at resistance would be suicide. Stealthily, other pirates swarmed into the wheelhouse and engine-room and took control of the ship. Mr. Lapsley, who had a good knowledge of Cantonese, was forced to act as an interpreter for the forty-strong band of pirates who had surreptitiously embarked at Amoy. The leaders of the pirates were well-informed and the reluctant interpreter had the risky job of telling them that no such bullion had been loaded at Shanghai and, at the prompting of Captain Pringle, it was made clear that a British warship was on its way to meet the ship. Angrily the pirates bustled Captain Pringle and Second Mate Hurst onto the bridge, threatening them with death if they did not navigate the ship into Bias Bay. With a sense of foreboding, the two men obeyed and when the pirates doused the ship's steaming lights and robbed and murdered some of the richer passengers, they knew they were extremely vulnerable.

Mr Beatty, the chief officer, found himself locked in his cabin, whilst Second Engineer Orr and Third Engineer Duncan, together with the lady passenger, were locked in the saloon. Chief Engineer Cormack was manhandled into the engine-room and told to keep the engines going, and for several hours the *Sunning* maintained a steady course southward. On the bridge, Captain Pringle and Second Officer Hurst found they were free to use the chartroom to plot the ship's position and John Hurst resolved to slip away in the darkness to the officers' cabins. His heart thumping wildly, he hurried to his own cabin and grabbed his Colt revolver. The chief officer's cabin door was next door and he kicked this open. Mr Beatty emerged, grasping a rifle – it was the point of no return.

However, in a further act of bravado, he found time to dive into his friend, William Orr's, cabin and collect the other Colt revolver. Thrusting both revolvers into his belt and stuffing the pockets of his tunic with ammunition, the second officer calmly returned to the bridge whilst Chief Officer Beatty crept off to release the others who were locked in the saloon.

His full account of what happened later appeared under the headline

'TABLES TURNED ON PIRATES
SECOND OFFICER'S STORY'

The Straits Times, 19th November 1926.

Captain James Pringle was immensely relieved to see the shadowy figure of John Hurst reappear at his side. He had been able to conceal a heavy cylindrical sounding lead in his jacket and had been determined to crack at least one pirate skull if his second officer had not returned. The two men urgently whispered a plan of action as the light on Chilang Point came into view. This excited the pirates who knew then that Bias Bay was not far off. The second officer surreptitiously took the sounding lead from the captain and as the Chinese came into the chartroom, he struck him with a strong blow to the back of his head, killing him instantly. The second officer then drew his revolvers and started firing.

Down below and hearing shots from the bridge, Chief Officer Beatty led his party out of the saloon and up the inside companionway to join in the fray. A pirate appeared and was brained with such force by his rifle that the weapon broke in two as they forced their way onward. The steel security gates, to which the pirates obviously had their own key, were re-locked and just after midnight the five British officers and Madame Prokieva entered into a life or death struggle with a band of blood-thirsty pirates.

Once the security grilles were locked, the bridge was impregnable and as long as their ammunition held out they were safe. During the next hour, accurate shooting from John Hurst and William Orr accounted for a dozen pirates but from then on they conserved their ammunition. Unaware of this, the pirates set fire to the accommodation beneath the bridge in a bid to flush the officers out, and soon a choking smoke made them cough and splutter. Chief Officer Beatty was shot and wounded but nobody noticed in the commotion. The engine-room stokehold crew fled from their posts and hid under the fo'c's'le head and, with no-one stoking the boilers, the ship gradually lost way and began to drift aimlessly.

Seizing the initiative and showing a sense of good seamanship, Captain Pringle directed his megaphone forward and bellowed an order to the Chinese bosun to let go the anchors. This was done and at once the ship swung round head to wind and the flames that were licking the bridge were swept away aft. Knowing that the Royal Navy was in the vicinity, the pirates realized that a ship on fire was bound to attract attention and they prepared to flee. Suspicious of the lull in hostilities, William Orr crept aft to reconnoitre and saw the pirates frantically lowering two lifeboats. Taking careful aim, he coolly shot one of them dead and then retreated back to the bridge. The pirates produced their interpreter who nervously pleaded for a cease-fire; the tables had been turned on the pirates and Captain Pringle shrewdly allowed them to leave as he turned his attention to saving the ship. The wireless operator wasted no time in tapping out an SOS and in the engine-room steam was raised and the fire hydrants began to spurt water as the crew tackled the flames.

All the lifeboats, with the exception of one, had either been damaged or taken by the pirates. As a precaution, Captain Pringle decided to lower it and to tether it alongside by the painter. Following the tradition that the first lifeboat lowered from a distressed ship is manned by the junior officers, Second Officer Hurst and Third Engineer Orr found themselves in charge. Madame Prokovieva joined them and while the Chinese women and children were being mustered to take their places, the painter became scorched, it then snapped and the lifeboat shot away into the early morning gloom.

The fierce fire which had gutted the midships cabins was gradually brought under control and in the early dawn the shape of a warship was seen rapidly closing on the *Sunning*. Soon the white hull and buff funnel of the sloop HMS *Bluebell* were clearly visible and, within the hour, an armed party of British matelots stormed on board. A search revealed some suspected pirates to be mixing with the deck passengers, but these were soon arrested. Leaving an armed party behind, HMS *Bluebell* sped away in pursuit of the pirates, capturing one boatload although the other with the hapless interpreter on board escaped. As back-up for *Bluebell*, three other H.M. ships, the *Vindictive*, *Despatch* and *Verity*, along with four seaplanes from *Hermes*, arrived to offer assistance.

Second Officer Hurst and Second Engineer Orr and their women passengers were picked up later by a Norwegian freighter, transferred to *Verity* and eventually landed at Hong Kong.

Meanwhile, the smoke-blackened and bullet-scarred *Sunning* remained at anchor with her main engine broken down. The Royal Navy scoured the seas for the rest of the pirates but had to be content with a total of nineteen prisoners. Two months later, the scrupulous fairness of British justice found only six of these guilty of piracy and thirteen of them were set free, those guilty going directly to the scaffold. The *Sunning* was towed to Hong Kong harbour, reconditioned and put back into service. Her officers had known that by resisting the pirates they would risk death – it had been a calculated risk and showed the confidence they had that the Royal Navy would arrive in time to rescue them.

Chapter 5

Sudden Death in Buenaventura

Midsummer 1926, and Captain Robert White was back at his home town of Troon after commanding the S.S. *Ashworth* on a 15-month around-the-world voyage. He had been born there in 1867 and loved the beautiful views of Arran, Ailsa Craig and the Ayrshire coast and liked to wander around Troon Harbour as he had done as a boy. On this particular leave, he was faced with making a difficult decision. After seven years employed with Dalgleish & Co., tramp ship owners of Newcastle, he had been offered the command of the S.S. *Tritonia* of the Donaldson Line of Glasgow. Although the Donaldson Line maintained regular services to South America and the United States and eastern Canada, they had several steamers in the deep sea tramping trade. The *Tritonia* was one of these and as Captain White enjoyed the independence that tramp ship skippers were given, he decided that a change of shipping companies would do him no harm.

Captain White was aged sixty and was in the enviable position of being comfortably off. He notified Dalgleish & Co. that he would be resigning and then spent the next six months relaxing at Troon before joining his new command at Glasgow in February 1927. The first person to welcome him on board was Alexander Johnston, the ship's young chief engineer. Alex Johnston was from Kilmarnock and a fine engineer whose outstanding qualities had quickly earned him promotion with the Donaldson Line. By the age of thirty he had been appointed chief engineer of the *Tritonia* and had been with the ship for the past five years. In the following sixteen months Captain White came to know his chief engineer very well, and after a long voyage the *Tritonia* arrived back in the UK on 1st June 1928. Once again Captain White found himself back at Troon, but given less than a month's leave, he began to feel weary of the seafaring life and was somewhat reluctant to resume command of the vessel. He convinced himself that perhaps his next voyage would be his last, and he rejoined the ship at Tilbury.

Empty of cargo, the *Tritonia* lay in the Thames whilst the Donaldson Line finalized an outward voyage that would send the ship towards the west coast of the United States where, using their long-standing connections, a homeward cargo could easily be found. On this voyage it was also planned to dry-dock the ship in Japan for routine maintenance. On 28 June the orders to sail finally arrived. The *Tritonia* was to load coal at Methil in Fifeshire for Port Said, but where she was bound after that was anybody's guess. In the event, after discharging at Port Said, she went through the Suez Canal to the fly-blown Eritrean (Ethiopian) port of Massawa to take on a cargo of salt for Calcutta. From Calcutta she took coal back around the Indian coast to Marmugoa, and then back to Calcutta in ballast. Loading low grade coal again, she headed eastward to Manila and then, again in ballast, she arrived at Nagasaki for dry docking. After spending Christmas in Japan, freshly painted and looking like a new ship, she waited for a cargo to take her across the Pacific.

The weeks passed and with no suitable cargo forthcoming, the Donaldson Line reluctantly ordered the ship to sail in ballast for Vancouver. Captain White and the ship's company presumed that they were to load a staple cargo of Canadian grain or timber for the UK and, from that point, it looked like being a straightforward voyage home. However, just two days out from Japan on 1st January 1929, Captain White was surprised to receive a wireless message that was to change everything. He was to proceed to Grays Harbour in Washington State instead of Vancouver. Unhappy with their steamer spending so much time in ballast, the Donaldson Line had seized the opportunity of an unusual short-term charter in order to recoup some of their lost profit. Captain White was pleased with this development because a gainfully employed ship would benefit everyone. Further details were received by wireless and he learnt that the *Tritonia* was to be chartered to the Winge Line for one round trip from the USA to Chile. He discussed this with Chief Officer Adam Jones and they agreed that the charter would be a busy one. At the age of fifty-three, Jones had been a chief officer with various companies for the past fifteen years, but was a relative newcomer to the Donaldson Line. It would be his responsibility to stow the various parcels of cargo as they were loaded, as well as ensuring that they would be accessible for discharge when required. It really was an art to stow assorted cargo, rather than the usual bulk cargoes of coal, salt, grain, sugar or ore in which tramp ships usually specialized.

After a twenty-day passage across the North Pacific, the *Tritonia* berthed at a cold and dreary Grays Harbour. It was soon obvious that the ship was to load an assortment of cargo, some of which required careful handling. To facilitate matters the Donaldson Line had sent their marine superintendent from Vancouver to advise on the best way of loading. As soon as the gangway was down he came straight on board. A conference was held when, amongst other things, the loading of 1,000 tons of high explosives at Dupont was discussed. The Donaldson Line seldom, if ever, carried explosives in their ships and this consignment was of some concern to Captain White. Neither he nor Chief Officer Jones had any experience of dealing with such a large amount of explosives, but the superintendent assured them that all would well.

There was little rest for the crew as the *Tritonia* was sent on a hectic round of loading at Portland, Vancouver, Seattle, Tacoma and Dupont. The cold winter weather had taken its toll and Captain White became ill with bronchitis. Her holds almost full and with a deck cargo of heavy cedar logs, the tramp ship eased alongside the solitary, snow-covered wharf that belonged exclusively to the Dupont Explosive Works. In addition to his normal duties, Chief Officer Jones had assumed command of the vessel and he was now faced with the task of correctly stowing the explosives which consisted of several thousand wooden cases of dynamite and hundreds of steel kegs of dynamite. Experienced shore gangs used the ship's derricks to ease the explosives gently into the tween-decks of no. 3 hold. This small hold was just forward of amidships and extended under the officers' saloon and the captain's cabin. Dupont's own inspector eventually gave the seal of approval that the explosives had been stowed according to the regulations, the hatch was closed and notices forbidding smoking anywhere near the hold were posted. The *Tritonia* was then cleared to sail for San Francisco and Los Angeles where even more cargo was waiting for her. The Winge Line's organization was very efficient and the various cargoes had been loaded without delay.

After a five-day voyage southward, the ship called into San Francisco and found a consignment of 1000 kegs of gunpowder, cases of dynamite, blasting caps, fuel oil and general goods waiting. She then spent one day at San Pedro harbour in Los Angeles loading drums of kerosene and gasoline, this last consignment fitting in with little space to spare. The Winge Line certainly knew how to load their ships fully and finally the deeply-laden *Tritonia* sailed for the west coast of South America.

It was baking hot in the afternoon on 27th February 1929 when the ship approached the Colombian port of Buenaventura. The pilot came on board and took up a position in the box-like wheelhouse of the *Tritonia*. A red flag was flying from the ship's signal mast which was the international signal displayed when a vessel was loading or discharging explosives. With this in mind, Captain White asked the Colombian pilot how far from town the ship was to be anchored. The pilot's reply was non-committal, but taking charge of the vessel he ordered a reduction in speed and took the ship into harbour. Buenaventura is situated on a small island and it was the practice for ocean-going ships to anchor in the shallow waters of the picturesque harbour and discharge into lighters. It was an out-of-the-way port of call for British ships and neither Captain White nor Chief Officer Jones had been there before. On the fo'c's'le head, the chief officer stood by to hear the order to let go the anchor, and became concerned when he realized that the pilot was taking the ship quite close to the town. When the anchor was let go, the *Tritonia* lay only about one mile south-west of the harbour. It was 6 pm and, as evening closed in, a bright red light was substituted for the red flag as the lights of Buenaventura flickered on.

Early the next morning the crew worked with a will to open all five hatches and position a forest of derricks for working cargo. By 8 am the gangs of shore labourers were clambering up the starboard gangway, chattering and laughing and smoking their strong-smelling cigarettes. Colombian customs officers had already positioned themselves at the head of the ladder and were making sure that all cigarettes were out. Chief Officer Jones also posted his own notices saying *No fumar* around the hatches and made sure that everyone was aware that explosives were on board.

Soon the harbour tug had a lighter alongside and slings of cargo were being hoisted out of the holds and swung over the side. There were ten cases of dynamite for Buenaventura and arrangements were made to take them ashore separately later in the day. It was understood that after discharging was complete, the loading of coffee would commence and the *Tritonia* would sail for Guayaquil that evening.

There was a busy day ahead for the ship's officers. Mr. McDougall, the third officer was put in charge of discharging the cargo from holds 1, 2 and 3, and Mr. McNie, the second officer, took charge of holds 4 and 5. Because the dynamite was in the tween-deck of no. 3 hold, Wireless Operator Cox was pleased to help the third officer by spending the day down in no. 1 hold. These officers were there to keep an eye on the stevedores, to watch for furtive smokers and to deter broaching or stealing from the cargo. Third Officer McDougall spent most of his time in no. 3 tween-deck where a valuable consignment of dressed timber was to go ashore before the dynamite. As for Chief Officer Jones, he was fully occupied seeing that the correct cargo came out of each hold according to the detailed and rather complicated stowage plan.

The day wore on and at 2.30 pm Captain White stood on the bridge wing dressed in his uniform whites. He was waiting for a launch to take him ashore because it was a master's duty to produce the ship's papers in every port. He gazed around. He was not particularly interested in the assortment of buildings that he had seen in so many ports. It was the background noises of clattering winches and foreign shouts and the mixed smells of cargoes that had become a part of his life. He reflected that he had been at sea for forty-seven years and realized that he still enjoyed it. Troon would have to wait. In no hurry to get ashore and absorbed in his thoughts, Captain White was slow to realize that something was amiss around no. 3 hatch. The next thing he knew was that someone was pounding up the bridge ladder and he turned to see the third mate hurrying towards him, shouting that there was a fire in no. 3 hold and that the dynamite was burning!

Telling the officer to sound the fire alarm, Captain White hurried down to see what was going on. The blood-curdling shriek of the steam whistle echoed around the harbour as Third Mate McDougall tugged hard on the lanyard sounding the whistle over and over again and from the fo'c's'le head came the frenzied clanging of the ship's bell.

Smoke was curling out of no. 3 hold and, as word of the fire spread, the stevedores scrambled over the side like scared rabbits and began to cast off the lighter. Much to Captain White's dismay, members of the crew followed hard on the heels of the Colombians. The crew were well-practised in boat muster and fire drill and knew full well that the alarm was a call to fire stations and not a signal to abandon ship. The blaring ship's siren had unintentionally caused many people to think that the ship was about to blow up because the engineer officers, the firemen, the entire catering department and most of the seamen had left the ship.

Chief Officer Jones had taken charge of fighting the fire and with the bosun and two sailors struggled to rig up a hose to douse the flames. Much to his annoyance, there was nobody in the engine-room to turn on the water for the hydrant, and he hastily organized a human chain to pass buckets of water from the galley across the deck and down into the hold. It was a forlorn task throwing half-full buckets of water onto cases of dynamite, and Second Mate McNie and Third Mate McDougall struggled to pull those cases that were smoking clear of the rest. Captain White, Wireless Officer Cox and Apprentice Levack stayed on deck and helped to pass the buckets of water.

To those in the hold the sight of the burning dynamite was terrifying. Some cases on the top tier were smoking at their seams and tongues of blue flame were flickering out. The donkeyman, Antonio Deas, miraculously appeared and the captain asked him where the chief engineers and other officers were. When Captain White learned that they were on the lighter and unable to return because the rope was cut, Antonio Deas was ordered below to provide water on deck.

A few minutes later the hose swelled and quivered as water under high pressure surged along its length. Down in the hold, Chief Officer Jones blasted the cases of dynamite with a torrent of water. A thick yellow smoke began to fill the hold, sparks flew and flames that had been beaten down came back to life as the water swept over them. The heat and choking fumes assailed the senses as well as the nerves of those fighting the fire and the realization that the hose was having no effect on the flames convinced Chief Officer Jones that it was futile to continue. He told McNie and McDougall to get out and he followed them up on deck.

The sudden appearance of the three officers, coughing from the effects of the fumes, was enough for Captain White to know that there was nothing else that could be done. He gave the order to abandon ship and those who had bravely remained on board (nine in number) hastily set about lowering a lifeboat when a harbour launch was seen coming up under the stern. Desperately they waved and yelled to this launch to go round to the lowered starboard gangway and then hurried down to meet it. Deftly, the launch came to the foot of the ladder and they tumbled aboard it, only Captain White hesitating, torn between staying with his ship or going ashore. Urged by those in the launch to hurry, he pushed the launch off and jumped in. Speeding away from the *Tritonia* he could not believe what was happening. Looking back, the ship's paintwork gleamed in the sun and coloured signal flags flapped gaily in the breeze. Only the faint plume of yellowy smoke rising up between the funnel and the bridge marred it.

Heading towards Buenaventura town, the launch was met by a more official launch carrying the captain of the port. Captain White was requested to change launches and he was then whisked away. Uneasily aware that if the *Tritonia* blew up much of the town could be destroyed, the Colombian port officials formally instructed Captain White that he must return and scuttle his ship. (The port authorities had already ordered their gunboat to sink the *Tritonia*, but it was out of action.) Without hesitation Captain White agreed to try. The harbour was shallow and if the *Tritonia* could be scuttled there was every chance that she could be saved and re-floated. The launch took him over to the harbour tug where many of the crew had clustered and were apprehensively watching events unfold. Coming alongside, Captain White asked Chief Engineer Johnston and Second Engineer Hall if they would come back on board with him to scuttle the ship. They both agreed and boarded the launch which took them back towards the smoking *Tritonia*. Knowing that their lives were at risk, all were silent and tense. The Colombian coxswain slammed the launch into reverse as he approached the bottom of the gangway and Chief Engineer Johnston said to the captain that there was little point in his coming on board as well. It made sense, Captain White had never been in the engine-room and did not know a seacock from a discharge valve.

The two officers jumped onto the ladder and ran up it and the coxswain wasted no time in gunning the launch clear. The two engineers disappeared from view. After what seemed an eternity, but was in reality only about five minutes, the two men appeared at the top of the ladder, gave a thumbs up, and started down. The motor of the launch roared into life when a mighty explosion ripped the *Tritonia* in half, blasting debris skywards. Captain White was thrown into the bottom of the launch and instinctively stayed there. He felt the heat of the blast sweep over him and did not expect to survive as great waves

The S.S. Tritonia.

struck the launch and violently spun it around. Amazed that he was still alive, Captain White risked a look over the gunwale. The *Tritonia* had almost disappeared – all that was left of her was a piece of the bow that protruded above water.

In Buenaventura, afternoons were a time of siesta, and most people had little notion of the drama taking place in the harbour. The fire in the hold had started at about 3 pm and the ship had exploded at 3.47 pm. The force of the blast smashed windows and doors, and fragments of hot metal peppered many rooftops. Along the waterfront, a rumour spread of further explosions and it was into this mixture of fear and anger that Captain White was now plunged. Together with the Colombian coxswain he stumbled ashore. He was dazed and deafened, his white uniform tattered and torn and he could hardly stand upright. He was promptly arrested by a squad of soldiers with fixed bayonets, who marched him off and flung him in prison. After much diplomatic activity he was released after eleven days.

The heroic deaths of Chief Engineer Alex Johnston and Second Engineer William Hall impressed the Colombians who later erected a monument in their memory. They were also honoured by King George V who posthumously awarded them the Albert Medal.

'Both, fully aware of the serious risk, sacrificed their lives
in a heroic attempt to prevent the explosion'.
Official citation, 4th March, 1930.

Captain White never recovered from his ordeal and on his return home accepted that the time had come for him to retire. He knew that he owed his life to that kind, last-minute thought by Alex Johnston.

Chapter 6

Nous Maintaindrons

MS *Suffolk,* flagship of the China fleet, was returning to Hong Kong after a lengthy patrol to Shanghai and the Yangtze delta. The *Suffolk's* motto was *Nous maintaindrons* (we will maintain) and the powerful warship and her complement of seven hundred men was steadfast in maintaining the security of the British Empire. On the voyage towards Hong Kong, the heavy cruiser had smashed her way southwards through typhoon weather – her excellent sea-going qualities meant that her quadruple screws could drive her at 30 knots in practically any conditions.

The sheltered waters of Hong Kong were reached as scheduled on Thursday, 4th October 1934, and the *Suffolk* tied up to a buoy in readiness to go alongside for a refit. A typhoon warning was hoisted in the harbour and moving the warship was delayed. On Saturday, a British freighter, the S.S. *City of Cambridge* wirelessed that she had grounded on Pratas Reef, and was in urgent need of assistance. The *Suffolk,* with steam on short notice, was ordered to slip her moorings and immediately put to sea to go to the rescue of the merchant vessel. She was soon crashing into restless seas and suffered some superficial damage when her commander, Captain Errol Manners, RN reluctantly conceded that the sea was rather rough and reduced speed to 25 knots!

The Pratas Reef lies about 180 miles south-east of Hong Kong. It is directly on the sailing route between Manila and Hong Kong, and from the Formosa Strait to the Strait of Singapore. It is a notoriously dangerous hazard to navigation and consists of a ring-shaped coral atoll that encloses a shallow lagoon. The atoll is about 13 miles across and has an opening on the western side, close to which is a small sandy island with a lighthouse. During the typhoon season, strong currents set with the wind and act like a strong magnet drawing any ship that is to windward onto the reef. Over the years, the Pratas Reef has been the graveyard of many ships, enough to make it worthwhile for Chinese fishermen to shelter in the lagoon for the purpose of looting wrecked vessels.

The S.S. City of Cambridge. *Grounded on the notorious Pratas Reef in the South China Sea, it was too dangerous for the crew to leave the ship. A British cruiser was quickly sent from Hong Kong to rescue them.* Photograph courtesy of V.H. Young and L.A. Sawyer, New Zealand.

In the early hours of Sunday, off the southern edge of the Pratas Reef, the keen eyes of *Suffolk*'s lookouts reported the masthead lights of a ship. Gleaming like pinheads in the dark, they were confirmed as the *City of Cambridge*. Although wireless contact was loud and clear, Captain Manners decided that he needed his own intelligence before making any decisions. The first light of dawn revealed the stationary silhouette of the freighter perched high up on the reef's edge and, from a distance, white flashes of surf could be seen thrashing up against the ship's side. To those on board the *Suffolk* the stranded ship presented an incredible sight. Caught in the grip of an immense swell, she had been lifted up and dumped squarely on top of the coral edge of the atoll leaving her rudder and propeller completely exposed. The starboard side was exposed to the crashing waves and the port side faced the calm of the lagoon. She was on an even keel and, to outward appearances, was undamaged.

From the foretop of the *Suffolk* the turquoise water inside the reef looked invitingly calm and Captain Manners resolved to send the boats in to assess the situation. Keeping to leeward of the fearsome reef he took the warship around to the western side towards the lighthouse and, coming in as close as he dared, he tentatively dropped anchor about a mile from the entrance channel that led into the lagoon. A motorboat towing a whaler was prepared and, in addition to the boats' crew, two lieutenant-commanders and the commissioned shipwright were to go to the wreck and report on the prospects of salvage. It would almost be a 30-mile round trip, but the mile from ship to shore would be the most dangerous part of the venture.

Captain Reginald Teague, master of the *City of Cambridge,* watched the arrival of the warship with relief. It was comforting to know that the Royal Navy was close at hand and communication was soon established by wireless and signal lamp. Everything had happened so quickly it was hard to believe that it was only at 5 am the day before that the Ellerman Line freighter, loaded with a general cargo from San Francisco en route for Hong Kong, had run onto the Pratas Reef. This was directly caused by several days of leaden skies and heavy rain making it impossible for Captain Teague to fix his position. (Captain Teague was later exonerated by a Court of Marine Inquiry held at Hong Kong).

Captain Teague had three main responsibilities. Firstly, he was concerned with the crew's safety; secondly he learnt that salvage tugs were on their way from Hong Kong, although he doubted that salvage was possible; and thirdly, a gang of ostensibly Chinese fishermen had appeared and threatened to take possession of the ship as soon as she was abandoned.

Braving the heaving ocean swells, the motorboat and the whaler disappeared into the entrance channel, anxiously watched by the warship's company. The placid lagoon was deceptive for although it was shallow, it was full of sharp, hidden rocks, 'sprinkled about like currants in a plum pudding' (*Ship's Magazine*, 1933–35, p.87). In places the water was less than three feet deep and the crews had to drag the boats forward. Two miles short of the *City of Cambridge* the motorboat was left with only the whaler being able to get close to the stranded ship. Captain Teague and his officers waded out through the knee-deep water to help them.

The Royal Navy experts decided that any hope of salvaging the merchant ship was impossible. From a sense of duty to the ship's owners, Captain Teague would not abandon the ship although he requested that her crew be taken off and, having accomplished their task, they returned to make their report. Captain Manners conveyed his impatience to Captain Teague with a message that he must use his own lifeboats to bring the crew off, for the *Suffolk* could not be expected to remain precariously at anchor for any longer than absolutely necessary. Captain Teague accepted this and the following morning most of the ship's crew of seventy Indian seamen and fourteen British officers hauled the two port lifeboats through the shallows to be towed out to the waiting warship. This operation was successful although twenty of the crew, including the captain,

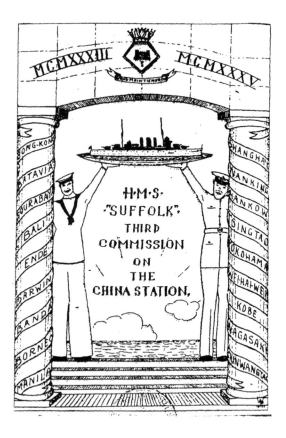

Shipboard publication of H. M. S. Suffolk, *motto Nous maintaindrons, which gives an interesting account of the rescue of the crew from the City of Cambridge.* Illustration courtesy of the Imperial War Museum.

had to wait until the next day to take their places. Captain Manners did not wish to spend another nerve-racking night at anchor just a mile off the reef, and made it clear to Captain Teague that the Admiralty and the Ellerman Line expected both himself and the remaining crew to be taken off on the morrow.

It was not long before the rescue of the ship's crew was complete the following day, with Captain Teague being the last to leave the freighter. As he did so, he was watched by a gang of Chinese fishermen who were intent on boarding and looting as soon as the ship was abandoned. It was after midday when Captain Teague in trilby hat and civilian clothes stood on the main deck of the *Suffolk* and shook hands with an impeccably white-uniformed Captain Manners. An hour later, her mission successfully completed, the cruiser weighed anchor and sailed for Hong Kong. The *City of Cambridge* was beyond salvage and a few months later, as the result of a feud between two gangs of looters, the ship and the remains of her cargo were set alight. The strange sight of a merchant ship stuck high and dry on a reef was seldom seen as navigators gave the Pratas Reef the widest possible berth.

Four and a half months after the rescue, the *Suffolk* came to the close of her two-year commission on the China Station. The ship's company was drawn up on the quarter-deck on 29th March 1935 to hear a farewell speech given by Admiral Sir Frederick Dreyer, Commander-in-Chief of the China Station. Among many other notable deeds, the admiral acknowledged the superb seamanship displayed by all concerned in the rescue at Pratas Reef, and he had great pleasure in presenting to *Suffolk* a silver tray on which were inscribed the words:

Presented to
The Captain, Officers and Ship's Company of
H.M.S. *Suffolk*
by
Ellerman's City Line of Glasgow
as a token of their great appreciation
of the very gallant services rendered to
the officers and crew of
S.S. *City of Cambridge*
Stranded on Pratas Island, October 1934.

Chapter 7

Call the Master!

S
loping gradually into the Caribbean Sea, Point Beata is the southernmost point of Hispaniola. Close by is the small but steep Beata Island, and 6½ miles to the south-west of Beata Island is the smaller island of Alta Vela. There is a deep water channel between the two islands called the Alta Vela Channel, which enabled ships to save several hours of valuable steaming time if a master chose to use it.

Alta Vela Island, rocky and only three-quarters of a mile long and half a mile wide, is composed almost entirely of a remarkable bell-shaped hill, the summit of which is 500 feet above high water. In addition, high on the rock was a light tower and, on a clear night, the light could be seen 15 miles away. In fact, Alta Vela Island was an excellent point of departure for vessels bound either east (towards the Atlantic) or west (towards the Panama Canal). There is only one hazard in the Alta Vela Channel and that is a low, flat, unlit rock, fringed with coral and sited half a mile from the northern side of Alta Vela Island. The rock was well-known to navigators and, on a dark squally night, a prudent skipper might elect not to pass through the 6-mile channel with its lurking rock and heavy swells, but decide to steam the extra miles by passing to the south of Alta Vela Island. The rock in question had the rather sinister name of Black Rock.

In 1935 the London-registered S.S. *Iddesleigh* was eight years old but still a modern, well-equipped cargo ship. She belonged to the Tatem Steam Navigation Company which had, over the years, built up good connections at Vancouver and their fleet of ten ships was often running on charter to and from the Pacific coast of Canada. In particular, the *Iddesleigh* was kept busy on round voyages from the United Kingdom to Vancouver, even though freight rates were low.

The Tatem tramp ships were easily distinguished by their efficient, utilitarian appearance and by their tall black smokestacks with the distinctive white T in a red band. The five holds of the *Iddesleigh* could carry 9,000 tons of cargo, her engines gave her an economical speed of 10 knots and she carried a crew of thirty-six hands. She was a fine ship and was owned and operated by one of Britain's better tramp companies from their head office at Bute Street, Cardiff.

During the glorious early May of 1935, the ship was at Vancouver taking on wheat for the flour mills of London. When her lower holds were full, she was required to load timber at three ports. Firstly she called at nearby New Westminster, and then across to the east coast of Vancouver Island to the small timber port of Chemainus. After two days there, she went through the strait of Juan de Fuca towards the rugged Pacific coast of the island to top off her timber cargo at the remote pulp and sawmill town of Port Alberni. This town lay at the end of the breathtakingly-beautiful Alberni Inlet, where dense pine forests stretched as far as the eye could see. The final consignment for the *Iddesleigh* was 900 tons of planks which were to be carried as deck cargo on the fore and aft decks. The ship's officers and the Canadian waterside workers were well versed in the art of stacking timber and the ship was ready to sail on 15th May.

In the early thirties a worldwide slump in trade meant that a large number of tramp ships had been laid up. The Tatem Steam Navigation Co. was no exception and the officers and crew of the *Iddesleigh* were very much aware that they were fortunate to be employed. The deck and engineer officers remained relatively unchanged for successive voyages and, under the command of Captain John Tonge, the *Iddesleigh* was a happy ship. Chief Officer William Leaker, aged forty-four, was three years older than the captain and, although he had served as relieving master of the ship, he felt that in better times he would have had his own command long ago. Second Mate Robert Kane and Third Mate William Escudier, both aged twenty-five, were thankful to be at sea and were looking forward to sitting their master's and mate's certificates respectively.

As the day wore on, the deckhands worked under the direction of Chief Officer Leaker to have the ship ready for a 4.30 pm departure. The Port Alberni pilot came on board and the *Iddesleigh,* loaded with 9,160 tons of grain and timber, moved back along the Alberni Inlet. It had been a long day for Chief Officer Leaker who had supervised securing the deck cargo and preparing the ship for sea but he then had to stand by on the fo'c's'le head. Whenever a ship is required to anchor it is the chief officer who is in charge of letting go (and heaving up) the anchor, and invariably his position is on the fo'c's'le head whenever a pilot was on board. The *Iddesleigh* cautiously followed the flashing lights that marked the winding channel and it was late when the pilot was dropped and the tramp steamer began the two-week passage towards the Panama Canal.

The transit of the Panama Canal over and all formalities completed, the ship steamed through the breakwater entrance of Limon Bay and out into the Caribbean. As on previous voyages, arrangements had been made to take on bunkers at Port Royal, Jamaica and the *Iddesleigh* duly arrived there at midday on 5th June. She was alongside the coaling wharf for only six hours before sailing at 6.35 pm direct for London. The usual route from Jamaica to the English Channel was to take Moran Point Light (at the eastern tip of Jamaica) as the point of departure and then shape an easterly course, proceeding along the southern coast of Hispaniola towards Alta Vela Island. Course was then altered to pass through the Mona Passage between Hispaniola and Puerto Rico and then the great circle track across the Atlantic to Bishop Rock was followed – a fairly straightforward passage for seasoned navigators.

The bridge deck and the captain's cabin on the Iddesleigh *are clearly shown. On merchant ships this small area was a skipper's private territory and it was accepted that it was off limits to officers and crew.* Photograph courtesy of the National Maritime Museum, London.

It was just past midnight when Captain Tonge determined that the Morant Point Light was directly on the port beam at a distance of 16 miles, the perfect position to set a course of S 88°E towards Hispaniola. Twelve hours later, a noon sight on 6th June gave the ship's exact position of latitude 17° 41'N and longitude 74° 20'W. Alta Vela Island was 155 miles ahead, and Captain Tonge altered course by 5° to starboard in order to pass 10 miles to the south. It was apparent that the Alta Vela Light should be visible somewhere on the port bow at about 3 am.

The afternoon was hot, with a blustery easterly wind hitting the steamer on the nose and frequently causing seas to burst over the bow. Chief Officer Leaker spent a long time checking the lashings of the deck cargo and, satisfied that all was well, he relieved Second Mate Kane on the bridge at 4 pm. Captain Tonge had just taken an observation for longitude and asked Bill Leaker to check it. When this was done a fairly accurate dead reckoning position (a term for estimating a position when conditions made actual observations impossible) was plotted on the chart. The question of whether they would use the Alta Vela Channel or steam the extra miles by going south of Alta Vela Island was discussed, with Captain Tonge declaring that he would not go through the channel in the dark.

Captain Tonge set up his chaise longue outside his cabin on the bridge deck. It was a sheltered spot directly in front of his cabin windows where he could easily take a break from standing on the bridge. On merchant ships this deck was regarded as the master's private domain and was not used by anyone else. It was a windy night with patches of rain cloud racing across the darkening sky, but he was well-protected from the elements by the solid stack of timber deck cargo on no. 2 hatch. At about 11 o'clock John Tonge left the bridge to take a short nap and told Third Mate Escudier that when he handed over the watch at midnight he was to make sure the second mate called him as soon as the Alta Vela Light was spotted. Dozing off, he awoke with a start and found that it was only 1 am. The ship was pitching heavily, making the timber deck cargo creak loudly. He went up to the bridge and found Second Officer Kane peering into the darkness trying to catch a glimpse of the Alta Vela Light. He told him that it was a bit early for that, but had no reason to check if the third mate had passed on his order to be called as soon as the light appeared. After checking the course, he stressed that he expected to be called when the light did appear and returned to his chaise longue. His bridge deck was a cosy nook and the monotonous pounding of the engines combined with the pitching of the ship and the creaking timber lulled the captain to sleep.

Second Officer Kane continually swept the darkness ahead with his binoculars. He was rewarded at 2.30 am when he caught the faintest glimmer of a light on the starboard bow. He went up on the Monkey Island and counted the flashes together with the sailor on lookout. It was the Alta Vela Light. Using the voice pipe to check that the man on the wheel was holding course, he took a bearing and went into the chartroom to mark it on the chart. Having done that he went down to the bridge deck where he knew he would find Captain Tonge.

"Captain, I have picked up Alta Vela on the starboard bow."

To which Captain Tonge stirred and replied, "Keep the light half a point on the starboard bow."

Knowing that the course set earlier by the captain was to leave Alta Vela Island to port, the second officer queried the direction. Starboard was confirmed by the captain and Robert Kane returned to the bridge.

Second Officer Kane was well aware that stringent economy was the order of the day so he assumed that Captain Tonge was about to take the short cut through the Alta Vela Channel to save on running costs. Persistent rain showers obscured the light and it was not until 3.15 am that the second officer could take another bearing. Conscious that it was over half-an-hour since he seen the master, Second Officer Kane began to wonder if he should call him again. As the minutes ticked by he expected Captain Tonge to come and give the order to change course. The *Iddesleigh* was closing with the island but he hesitated to make any alteration of course, fearing that he would incur the captain's wrath. He chose to wait until the chief officer came on watch when it would be his responsibility.

Chief Officer Leaker arrived on the bridge just before 4 am. He sensed something was amiss because the second officer seemed immensely glad to see him. A curtain of rain was obscuring the Alta Vela Light but after poring over the chart and going by the second officer's bearings, he assumed that the vessel was steering a course into the Alta Vela Channel. Chief Officer Leaker was surprised that the master was not on the bridge as he knew that Captain Tonge did not intend to take the ship through the channel and would normally have been on the bridge.

Second Officer Kane left the bridge at 4.05 am and made his way down to his cabin. He was undressing and ready to turn in when the engine shuddered and stopped. He hurriedly dressed and returned to the bridge with a sense of foreboding.

Chief Officer Leaker hardly had time to wonder where Captain Tonge was when he glimpsed the dark shape of land perilously close on the port bow. His reaction was instantaneous. He shouted to the helmsman to turn the wheel hard-a-starboard, and then stopped the engine before throwing it into full astern. Having done that, he sprang down the ladder to the bridge deck and, finding Captain Tonge fast asleep on the chaise longue, yelled for him to get up. The two men raced up the ladder to the bridge, but before they reached it the *Iddesleigh* ran onto the rocky coral that fringed Black Rock.

The engine was kept going in reverse, but the tramp steamer was skewered by the bow and sea water flooded into the forepeak and no. 1 hold. The engine was stopped and, although the pumps were pouring out water at a tremendous rate, the water level in no. 1 hold continued to rise. The crew were set to work jetti-soning the deck cargo in order to clear no. 1 hatch, and when the hatch boards were thrown off a mess of waterlogged timber floating on 2,000 tons of sodden grain was revealed. To make matters worse, the tide was on the ebb and the swell in the channel made the bottom of the ship bump and grind on the coral. Any chance of refloating the *Iddesleigh* depended on lightening the forepart of the vessel and getting a tug to pull her free by the stern. An SOS directed to Jamaica brought a quick response and the powerful salvage tug *Relief* packed with pumps, steel plating, riveting and cutting gear and diving equipment left her home base of Kingston for a 30-hour dash to save the stricken steamer.

At 6.30 in the evening of 8th June, the massive tug (at 185 feet long she was almost half the length of the *Iddesleigh*) arrived on the scene. A four-day operation which involved jettisoning the bundles of timber from the murky water in no. 1 hold, fixing temporary patches to the outer hull and fastening a cumbersome towing cable to the steamer's stern, resulted in the *Relief* successfully dragging the steamer free. The *Iddesleigh* was then towed 18 miles to the north-west and anchored in the sheltered waters behind the red cliffs of False Cape (Hispaniola). A further sixteen days were spent using a steel scoop fabricated by the ship's engineers to dump much of the saturated grain overboard. Once this was done further patching and pumping enabled the ship to sail back to Kingston to be made watertight.

After a month in harbour, the *Iddesleigh* was given a certificate of seaworthiness and was permitted to sail for London, where she was dry-docked and extensively repaired after discharging. A Court of Marine Inquiry found that although Second Officer Kane had called the master, he had not made sure that Captain Tonge was fully awake. Captain Tonge and Second Officer Kane both had their certificates suspended which, in effect, terminated their careers. Chief Officer Leaker was dismayed to find that he was also held partly to blame for the stranding since he should have sent Second Officer Kane to call the master immediately.

Chapter 8

A Master Censured

Anchored off Keppel Harbour, it gave Captain John McLeod no pleasure to read about his ship in the afternoon newspaper.

'Steamer on reef holed in Singapore Strait.
Freighter arrives with heavy list'.

Straits Times, 13th January 1927

Only a few hours earlier he had been passing through the Singapore Strait without the slightest intention of calling into Singapore.

Captain McLeod would be forty in 1927 and he looked forward to many more years in command with the prestigious Blue Star Line. He had been master of the S.S. *Royalstar* for over two years and knew the characteristics of the vessel very well. He had spent countless hours on her bridge being responsible for the safety of his ship in restricted waters – one of which was the Singapore Strait. He had been up all night and in the early hours of 13th January, the *Royalstar* was approaching the eastern end of the Singapore Strait. He studied Admiralty chart No. 2403 and noted how the Horsburgh, Raffles and Sultan Shoal Lighthouses, as well as numerous lights and beacons, were perfectly placed to take the bearings needed to pass safely through. In the chartroom there was a copy of the *Malacca Strait Pilot,* 1924 edition which covered the Singapore Strait, but as he was satisfied with the chart, he did not use it.

At precisely 6.14 am Captain McLeod plotted the ship's position on the chart. The Horsburgh Lighthouse was on the port beam, 1 mile distant and the ship, loaded with 8,500 tons of frozen eggs and mutton, was making excellent speed through the calm waters. It had been five years since Captain McLeod had last passed through the Straits when he had been in command of the *Romanstar*, another Blue Star Line freighter. Having satisfied himself that all was well for the moment, he went below for breakfast and looked forward to spending the rest of the day on the bridge navigating the ship through the strait.

It was a glorious morning when Third Mate Thomas MacDonald came on watch at 8 am and joined Captain McLeod on the bridge. Away to starboard the shoreline was quite clear, and in about an hour the *Royalstar* would be passing the city of Singapore. These were busy waters and a good lookout had to be kept for steamers. Singapore was a regular port of call for the smart ships of the P & O, British India, Blue Funnel, Ben, Prince and Ellerman Lines as well as a host of tramp ships, but the Blue Star Line seldom called there. The *Royalstar* was homeward bound from Shanghai to London and would not be stopping.

South of Singapore and its dockland of Tanjong Pagar, the strait narrowed to 2½ miles with the St. John Islands and the Batu Beranti Shoals fringing the southern edge. Captain McLeod appreciated the fine weather and smooth sea because it was making the 60-mile long navigation of the strait a pleasure. At 9 am he set about taking his second bearings of the morning. He chose to use the centre of Peak Island to starboard and another of the light tower on the rocks of Batu Beranti to port, and by crossing these two bearings he could fix the exact position of the ship on the chart. The freighter was travelling at 11 knots and Captain McLeod went into the chartroom to plot the bearings, leaving Third Mate MacDonald alone on the bridge. However, Thomas MacDonald could see plainly that the light tower on Batu Beranti lay practically dead ahead at a distance of about 2 miles, and if he were in command he would ease the ship over to starboard. Ten minutes later Captain McLeod reappeared and quickly ordered the helmsman to ease the wheel over to starboard. The ship responded and began to swing towards the centre of the strait when there was a dull boom from low down on the starboard side, followed by a series of extraordinary hissing noises. Alarmed, Captain McLeod stopped the engines and allowed the *Royalstar* to lose way and gradually stop, by which time the ship's exact position had been marked on the chart.

At first it was unclear what had happened, and the hissing was attributed to a broken steampipe on the foredeck winches. However, it did not take the engineers very long to find the real cause. The hull had been punctured well below the waterline and the inrushing sea water had filled the double bottom tanks, forcing air up and out of the vent pipes on deck. This was confirmed when the vessel took on a starboard list and began to settle noticeably by the head. Hurried soundings of the bilges showed that holds 1 and 2 were dry and it appeared that only the outer bottom plates had been ruptured, presumably by a submerged object. There was no way of knowing just how badly the ship was damaged and, signalling that his ship was taking water, Captain McLeod took her 4 miles up the winding channel that led to Keppel Harbour. Her sudden arrival created a lot of interest and preparations were hurriedly made to put the vessel into King's Dry Dock. Just eastward of the dock were the Peninsular & Oriental Company's wharves where the vessels of that company berthed. It was the heart of Singapore's shipping and commercial district, and word soon spread of the unexpected arrival of a Blue Star freighter that appeared to be in danger of sinking.

As an anchorage, Keppel Harbour was indifferent and the harbour authorities rarely allowed a vessel to anchor except in special circumstances. Setting up the dry dock, which fortunately was empty, took time and the *Royalstar* spent twenty-four hours at anchor before being docked, when the full extent of the damage could be seen. Captain McLeod and his officers shook their heads in

The S.S Royal Star *(formerly the* Royalstar *1919–1930). Passing through the Singapore Strait, the ship hit an uncharted reef and, badly holed, managed to enter harbour and the safety of dry dock.*

disbelief. The curve of the starboard bilge, 28 feet below the water line, had been sliced open with the sharpness of a surgeon's knife from the bow to no. 2 hold, a distance of over 50 feet. If the ship had hit the object square on, then her bottom would have been sliced wide open. It had been a close call for the ship could have quickly filled and sunk. The Government Surveyor of Ships (Straits Settlements), Mr G. Herron, expressed the opinion that the *Royalstar* had certainly scraped along a reef and had been lucky not to have sunk.

Repairs would be extensive and at least two weeks would be needed to renew the shell plating, replace a buckled propeller blade and concrete the bilge. These repairs would only be temporary, allowing the ship to reach England for major work to be carried out. All her refrigerated cargo was transferred into cold storage ashore and life in King's Dry Dock became unbearable. On board a ship in dry dock, especially in the tropics, it is hot and stuffy and toilets and washrooms cannot be used. It was an uncomfortable time for the crew while Captain McLeod was waiting to be summoned to an impending formal investigation into the circumstances of the grounding of his ship.

On the morning of 25th January 1927, Captain McLeod and Third Officer MacDonald (as officer of the watch), escaped the fierce heat of Singapore and entered the cool portals of the District Court. They were to attend a Marine Inquiry into the circumstances of the grounding of the *Royalstar.* A district judge presided and was assisted by two master mariners. A solicitor appeared for the Crown and a solicitor represented Captain McLeod and Third Officer MacDonald. The crucial question focused on Captain McLeod – was the casualty caused by negligence, error of judgement or the unskilful navigation of John McLeod, master of the S.S. *Royalstar?* As the morning session unfolded and various statements and evidence were presented, it became apparent that the court was somewhat unsympathetic towards the captain.

After lunch the inquiry continued with some rigorous cross-examination. Mr. Seth, K.C., Solicitor General of Singapore and appearing for the Crown, quickly established that Captain McLeod had been on the bridge throughout, that the day had been fine and clear, and the captain had been using Admiralty chart 2403 to navigate the ship through Singapore Strait. Captain McLeod conceded that his chart was not as up-to-date as it could have been but, in his opinion, it was quite in order to use the chart to navigate the strait, since he was not actually calling into Singapore. Then came a question that made Captain McLeod feel hot under his stiff collar.

"Captain, on board your ship do you have a copy of the *Malacca Strait Pilot?*"

"Yes, there is."

"Captain, did you consult that book at any time before entering the Singapore Strait?"

Captain McLeod had been expecting that question and his answer was straightforward.

"No, I did not. The chart was sufficient."

However, Mr. Seth persisted with his line of questioning.

"Captain, I would like to read to you something from page 170 of that book ..." The lawyer held a copy of the *Malacca Strait Pilot* in his hand, it had only recently been published for the Admiralty Hydrographic Department by His Majesty's Stationery Office, and had been available to shipmasters since 1924. Mr. Seth opened the book at chapter VI, page 170, Singapore Strait.

> '**Batu Berhanti** *(Beranti), two rocky ledges, about 2½ cables apart, the centres of which are above water, lie a mile northward of Blaking Padang Light.*
> *A patch of 5 fathoms lies 2 cables northward of the western one, and a patch of 2 fathoms at 2¾ cables north eastward.*
> *A bank about 2½ miles long lies eastward of Batu Berhanti Light, with depths varying from 4¾ to 10 fathoms (Chart 2403).*
> **Eddies and overfalls** *– owing to the strong tidal streams which prevail in this part of the strait, and the rocky and uneven nature of the bottom, violent eddies and overfalls are usually to be met with; it is therefore advisable to keep on the north side of the strait.'*
>
> *Malacca Strait Pilot*, first edition, 1924

Mr. Seth repeated the final paragraph, closed the book, faced Captain McLeod and said,

"I think, Captain, that if you had read these directives, then you would have kept to the north side of the strait and avoided this dangerous region altogether."

To this assertion, Captain McLeod referred to his own chart, pointing out the position where the *Royalstar* had struck. It clearly showed the courses that had been steered and that the ship had been at least 1 mile away from Batu Beranti when she had hit something. The *Malacca Strait Pilot* made no mention of any dangers in that vicinity.

In Captain McLeod's favour was the fact that it was impossible to say whether or not the vessel had struck an uncharted rock. Examination of Admiralty chart 2403, marked with the latest corrections, showed no reef, shoal or hazards where the ship had grounded.

After a short adjournment, the court reconvened and gave their decision. The casualty was caused by the negligence of the master:

1. In omitting to satisfy himself personally that his charts were up-to-date.
2. In neglecting to read the instructions on page 170 of the *Malacca Strait Pilot*.
3. In neglecting to have any bearings taken, or the position fixed between 6.14 am and 9.05 am.

The court did not consider it necessary to suspend his master's certificate, but severely censured him for his negligence. Third Officer MacDonald was absolved from all blame.

Captain MacLeod was astounded. He had been found negligent, yet his master's certificate had been neither cancelled nor endorsed. How could he be blamed for his ship striking what was obviously an uncharted small pinnacle of rock? It was a hard verdict to accept. He returned to the *Royalstar*, his certificate unblemished, but his career irretrievably damaged.

With shipping queueing to enter the dry dock, the pressure was on to refloat the ship, reload her cargo from cold storage and send her on her way. Taking command for what he knew would be his last voyage with the Blue Star Line, Captain McLeod was glad to leave the heat, smells and memories of Singapore far behind him. He felt that the verdict of the Singapore Court had been unjust and he became determined to clear his name.

As soon as the *Royalstar* reached London, Captain McLeod was unemployed so he had time on his hands. Appealing against a decision made by a Court of Marine Inquiry was difficult and it was suggested that if there was a right of appeal, then it would have to be heard in the Supreme Court of the Straits Settlement in Singapore. The first step was to go to the High Court in London to seek leave to appeal and this was granted after legal examination of the Shipping Acts. The next stage was the appeal itself. This was held a year later in London where the High Court gave a judgement in favour of Captain McLeod.

> 'His Lordship could not find that in the circumstances the master was culpably negligent. He therefore came to the conclusion that the appeal should be allowed and the censure set aside'.

Captain McLeod had been vindicated. However, the Blue Star Line remained unmoved and he was not offered another appointment. After a gap of twelve years he took command of the run-down tramp S.S. *Starstone* of London, just five days after Britain declared war on Germany.

Chapter 9

Mr Instone's Gold Medal

The S.S. *Darius* was at Port Melbourne loading horses for Colombo, Madras and Calcutta. Her holds were being filled with sacks of oats, bran and chaff, as well as bale upon bale of compressed fodder. The dockside was loud with the neighing and squealing of horses as four hundred and fifty-seven of the nervous beasts had to be individually enticed or prodded up the sloping gangway. Standing watching all this activity was a small but sturdy elderly man. His name was Archibald Currie, he was a Scot and was the owner of the *Darius*.

In 1862, Captain Currie had established a shipping line in Melbourne and, by 1899, the Arch. Currie & Co's Australian and Indian Line had five steamships running regularly between Melbourne and Calcutta. The company held the premier position in the transportation of Australian horses to India. These ranged from remounts for the Indian Army to the supply of racehorses. To make the trade especially profitable, the ships were crammed with Indian produce for the return voyage to Australia. The Currie Line steamers were fitted out to carry in excess of five hundred horses, and sufficient fodder and water to keep them in top condition. Officers of the Currie Line were adept at loading and unloading the often highly-strung animals, and avoiding bites from horses was a skill quickly learnt.

Archibald Currie could see that his officers were well in control of the situation and he went on board to wish them a pleasant voyage. The captain of the *Darius*, Walter Frith, was genuinely pleased to see the owner of the company. He appreciated the fact that Captain Currie had done things the hard way and, although now a highly-respected businessman, would be away to sea if he had the chance. It was Friday, 21st July 1899 and the first of the thirty passengers were beginning to come aboard. The majority of them were horse attendants, but a handful were off to seek their fortunes in British India. Two young men in particular – Neeson and Wilson – were bold-spirited and ready for any adventure that came their way. The following day the *Darius* left the Port Melbourne pier bound for Colombo.

Captain Walter Frith had previously been master of another Currie Line steamer, the *Clitus*. He had assumed command of the larger and more modern *Darius* in November 1896, and had completed seven round trips to Indian ports since then. The outward route was east then north toward the Torres Strait, which provided an easier sea journey for the horses, calling at such ports as Surabaya, Batavia, Singapore, Rangoon, Calcutta, Madras and Colombo. The return voyage was always southward through the invariably rough seas and south-west monsoons of the Indian Ocean and the heavy weather often encountered crossing the Great Australian Bight.

Ten days after leaving Melbourne, the *Darius* had passed through Torres Strait, dropping the pilot off at Thursday Island on 1st August. Although the weather had been perfect, Chief Officer Upjohn was obliged to report that three horses had died. With Colombo as her first port of call, the *Darius* began the long crossing of the Indian Ocean. No land was seen for eight days until Christmas Island was sighted on 10th August. The voyage continued in perfect weather until 7.45 in the evening of 14th August, when loud crashing noises were heard from the engine-room, accompanied by terrible vibrations. The engines raced wildly until they were abruptly closed down and, in the deafening silence that followed, everybody waited apprehensively.

The sea was calm as the *Darius* lost way and stopped. Suspecting that the trouble lay along the tail shaft, the engineers entered the pitch-black shaft tunnel, using their lamps to find their way along to the stern gland. All was well, so it seemed likely that the outer end of the shaft had snapped and the propeller had been lost. The *Darius* started to roll gently in the long ocean swell and Captain Frith took advantage of a light breeze to set some makeshift sails to steady the ship. By morning the wind had dropped and, in spite of extra sails being improvised, the ship began to roll heavily. With the light of day it was confirmed that the shaft had indeed snapped, taking the propeller with it, so fitting a whole new end shaft at sea was out of the question. The only solution was to seek help from a passing steamer and request a tow. In expectation of this the distress flags 'NC' were hoisted at the foremast head, and the Red Ensign was flown upside down from the main mast.

At noon the ship's position was fixed by taking a meridian altitude of the sun, placing the sweltering *Darius* just south of the equator and approximately 700 miles from the west coast of Java. It was hoped she would drift into the track of steamers travelling from the Sunda Straits to Colombo and Aden, but there was no guarantee of that. In the meantime there was nothing to do except wait.

Another day followed with the ship pitching violently. It was decided to trail or drag a sea anchor, and a contraption was made out of tarpaulins lashed onto a stout triangular framework. This was weighted with chain and dropped over the stern. The device did dampen the pitching, but the heaving weight of the ship soon caused it to disintegrate. After five days of vainly scouring the horizon for steamers, and with four hundred and fifty-four horses on board, things began to look grim. The realization that the *Darius* was drifting out of the regular track of steamers and into an empty part of the ocean brought matters to a head. During the afternoon of 19th August, Captain Frith asked his officers if anyone would care to skipper a ship's lifeboat and go in search of assistance. He had hardly finished speaking when Second Officer Reginald Instone promptly volunteered to go.

Second Officer Instone's mission was to make towards Padang on the Sumatran coast in the hope of intercepting a steamer and getting assistance. Once the decision to go had been made, five Indian seamen were chosen as boat's crew, and to give the second officer moral support two passengers, Messrs Neeson and Wilson, offered to accompany him. It was a venture fraught with danger which took courage to leave a perfectly sound ship and set off in an open boat 700 miles from the nearest land.

The *Darius* carried six lifeboats and once one was selected it was stocked with bags of biscuits, tinned provisions and many bottles of water. In all, enough to last eight men for at least thirty days. In addition, a box of blue signal rockets, lamps and oil, soap, buckets, wood and tools, a compass, navigational instruments, binoculars, a loaded revolver and a large Red Ensign were placed in the boat. Captain Frith handed the second officer a note of the ship's most up-to-date position and a chart of the west coast of Sumatra. Wishing each other good luck, the two men walked out to the starboard boatdeck where the lifeboat was swung out and waiting. The evening was perfect and the sea smooth as the lifeboat was gently lowered and it pulled away from the ship with a few strokes of the oars. The lug sail was hoisted and with Second Officer Instone at the helm, the lifeboat left the security of the *Darius* and bobbed away into the gathering gloom.

At noon the next day, Second Officer Instone obtained a sight of the sun which gave him a latitude of 2° 37'S and he estimated the longitude as 91° 01'E. The lifeboat had travelled 66 miles from the *Darius* but there was over 500 miles of open ocean ahead. The fine weather allowed Neeson and Wilson to familiarise themselves with handling the tiller and confidence was high as the boat surged eastwards. There was cause for celebration the following day when the noon position showed that they had sailed 134 miles in twenty-four hours. The weather eventually changed into squalls and rough seas. The voyagers became drenched and seasick, and for the next two days the lifeboat struggled on under double-reefed canvas.

The weather did not improve; the rain increased in its ferocity. Tired and bedraggled, the eight men bailed for all they were worth while the lifeboat was flung wildly about. Reginald Instone had spent fourteen hours at the helm and,

Built in Sunderland for the Currie Line of Melbourne in 1892, the S.S Darius *traded between Australia and India. Here she flies the Currie house flag, white background with a broad blue St Andrew's cross with a red diamond in the centre. The funnel colours were a single thin white band on black.*Photograph courtesy of the Ian J. Farquhar Collection

utterly exhausted, he handed over the tiller to one of his companions whilst he struggled to stream a sea anchor over the bow. The rudder jumped from its pintles and the second officer immediately used the long steering oar to keep the boat's head into the seas. It was only due to his quick thinking that the boat did not capsize. When the boat suddenly sprung a leak, it seemed as if they were about to drown but at this critical point, Wilson's humour shone through, "Never mind, the water is warm!"

Unexpectedly, the weather eased and the leak was plugged with soap and the rudder dropped back into position. On the morning of 25th August the wind was once again blowing strongly and the lifeboat remained hove to. The blinding rain was incessant and it took all of Second Officer Instone's encouragement to keep everyone's spirits up. For five long days they had been buffeted about, but at every opportunity a course had been shaped to the east-nor-east. The sky remained overcast and it was not until noon on 27th August that a sight of the sun was able to be taken. The second officer had managed to keep the chart and his navigational instruments dry so he was able to record their position as being only about 150 miles from Pulo Bulo Island Lighthouse, situated just off the Sumatran coast.

The calm after the storm continued, so that for one whole day little progress was made as the lifeboat drifted idly. Taking advantage of any wisp of wind and urging the boat's crew to pull on the oars, Second Mate Instone coaxed the boat towards land. Early on the morning of 30th August a steamer was sighted which was eagerly signalled. The Red Ensign was hoisted upside down as a sign of distress but the steamer took no notice of them. Later in the afternoon the hazy outline of land was sighted which Second Officer Instone was able to identify as the western tip of Tanah Bala Island. To confirm this the flashing light of Pulo Bulo Island Lighthouse was seen that night. This light was visible from about 26 miles, and from Pulo Bulo it was only 120 miles to the port of Padang.

The night turned stormy and wet as the second officer steered a course that would take them through Siberut Strait, keeping the lighthouse on the port bow. The dawn revealed land opening up on either side of them and far ahead a steamer was spotted going south. When they failed to attract the attention of this ship, they reconciled themselves to sailing the boat all the way to Padang. However, seeing his crew cold and weary, Second Officer Instone headed for the lighthouse with the intention of landing, obtaining fresh food and making their plight known. The choppy seas and strong current made sailing towards Pulo Bulo Island difficult but they persevered. At 10.30 am they were alarmed to see a 20-foot long, yellow and black sea serpent swim under the stern of the boat. Their initial reaction was to shoot it with the revolver but, fearful of it turning and attacking the boat, they left it alone.

All day the lighthouse tantalizingly offered a safe haven but at 3 o'clock, defeated by contrary winds, Second Officer Instone gave up and put the lifeboat on an easier heading. During the night they left the lighthouse astern and settled down to sail to Padang. At 2 am a masthead light appeared ahead and, not wishing to miss any opportunity, a blue distress rocket was fired. This was answered and the steamer altered course and picked them up. She was the *Reael*, a small Dutch-registered coaster that was bound for Padang. Although elated at being on board, the eight men were sad to see their lifeboat cast off for there was no room on deck. Reginald Instone and his crew had spent twelve days and thirteen nights in the lifeboat, they had sailed over 600 miles and knew that they could have sailed on to Padang if necessary. It had been a tremendous example of bravery and seamanship.

Padang was one of the most attractive places in the Netherlands East Indies and was an important trade centre. It was connected by telegraph to Batavia and soon the predicament of the *Darius* had been transmitted throughout the East and masters of ships crossing the Bay of Bengal were requested to keep a lookout for her. Arrangements were made to send Second Officer Instone and his crew onward to a port in British India and, by good fortune, the light cruiser HMS *Phoenix* was about to leave Batavia for Singapore. After a dash across country, Reginald Instone and his crew were welcomed on board the cruiser which took them to Singapore. Another passage was then readily available on the S.S. *Arratoon Apcar* which was bound for Calcutta. After all their adventures they found themselves as passengers rounding the last reach of the Hooghly River into the heart of Calcutta where they saw the familiar shape of the *Darius* in the bustling harbour!

While Second Officer Instone and his crew had willingly risked their lives in the lifeboat, those on board the *Darius* had faced a very uncertain future. Drifting helplessly, the steamer slowly rolled and lurched her way into a patch of ocean which ships rarely crossed. In spite of experimenting with an array of makeshift sails it was impossible to steady the ship and the well-being of the horses became a major problem with the heat. In the early dawn of 23rd August a smudge of smoke appeared on the horizon. There was a hush of expectation as everyone on board waited to see if the smoke would come closer or disappear out of sight. The tension on board turned to joy when the smoke was seen to be coming closer and they began firing a series of distress rockets. There were loud cheers when the steamer was seen to alter course and come steadily towards them. She was the S.S. *Gulf of Ancud* of Greenock and was loaded with sugar on a voyage from Java to Cuddalore on the Madras coast. It was an out of the ordinary voyage and if she had not passed by on that day the chances of the *Darius* being found easily would have been slight.

The meeting took place at latitude 0° 17'S longitude 92° 23'E, which was almost on the equator and 900 miles south-east of Colombo. Captain Frith requested a tow, and after coming to an agreement about salvage, the master of the *Gulf of Ancud* agreed. The rest of the day was spent using lifeboats to run a towing hawser between the two ships and the tow began towards Colombo late in the afternoon. Belching black smoke from her funnel, the *Gulf of Ancud* needed extra revolutions to pull the heavy load. Much to the relief of those on board the *Darius,* once the tow had settled down to a steady 5 knots, the heavy rolling they had endured since the breakdown finally ceased.

Over the next week, high southerly swells tended to help the two vessels on their way, the towing hawser remained intact and numerous steamers were sighted on nearing Ceylon. On 29th August, the P & O liner *Oriental,* bound for Colombo, her decks lined with excited passengers, came up to them and exchanged flag signals. At 7.30 the next morning the Point de Galle was in sight and the following morning the two ships entered Colombo Harbour. The *Gulf of Ancud* had towed the *Darius* for seven days and eight nights for a distance of 942 miles.

Discharging the remaining horses and cargo began immediately. A further fourteen animals had died which, considering the circumstances, was not a heavy loss. There were no facilities at Colombo for dry-docking and fitting a propeller, so the engineers of the *Darius* set about doing the job themselves. With all the cargo out and the bunkers almost empty, the vessel was light and floated high out of the water. By filling her fore peak and forward ballast tanks with water the forepart of the vessel went down and her stern rose, exposing the propeller aperture. The broken section of shaft was withdrawn, a new one fitted and the spare propeller bolted into place. The *Darius* was then able to take on her cargo and complete her voyage.

Chief Officer Upjohn was checking the mooring lines of the *Darius.* The ship had completely discharged her cargo and was riding high against the quayside. Suddenly he heard some friendly shouts and looking down he saw a party of men coming up the steep gangway. It was Second Officer Instone followed by Neeson and Wilson and five lascar sailors. He hurried to welcome them back on board, and later was quoted as saying.

'I cannot say we felt keenly anxious about the safety of the boat's crew. We thought about them a good deal, of course, but we persuaded ourselves that Mr. Instone would accomplish his mission'.

The *Darius* spent some time in dry dock before loading a full cargo for Australia, and during that period the courage of Second Officer Instone and his crew became well-known in Calcutta. At a well-attended ceremony at the exclusive Shipmaster's Club, he was presented with a gold medal with the inscription –

> Presented to R.L. Instone
> Second Officer of the Steamship *Darius*,
> by Members of the Shipmasters' Club,
> Calcutta, 28th September 1899

On the reverse:

> For Distinguished Bravery
> in Sailing in an Open Boat
> 650 Miles for Assistance

Captain Frith, who had handled the *Darius* superbly whilst his vessel had been disabled, was also presented with a medal. Later, Second Officer Instone was awarded the highly esteemed Lloyd's of London silver medal for meritorious services.

In Melbourne, Captain Archibald Currie, the owner of the Currie Line, took note of the young second officer who had shown such initiative and daring and marked him down for promotion. Six years later, Captain Reginald Lyon Instone was master of the S.S. *Gracchus*, the Currie Line's newest ship.

Chapter 10

Roasted Maize

In 1928 W.H. Seager & Co. of Cardiff, known as the Tempus Shipping Company, owned a small fleet of tramp ships that was profitably employed carrying bulk cargoes. On 6th May 1928, after a three-month round voyage to Argentina, one of the fleet, the S.S. *Campus*, docked in her home port of Cardiff. Among those signing off was Mrs. Annie Therbyson, wife of the captain, and Mrs. May Houston, wife of the chief engineer. They had many yarns to tell their families and friends, for whom any prospect of foreign travel was unknown. The two women had taken excursions in Rio de Janeiro and Buenos Aires and had had the experience of a lifetime. They left the ship to return to their homes, but their husbands remained to see to the ship's business.

Thousands of tons of best Welsh steaming coal, consigned to Tenerife, cascaded into the ship's four main holds and, after only five days alongside, the *Campus* was underway again. To save on expenses, her bunkers were crammed with 1,426 tons of a lower grade coal, for tramp steamers did not have the luxury of burning the best. Careful calculations showed this coal would be enough to take her fully loaded to Tenerife, thence to Argentina in ballast and then, loaded with cereals, back to the bunkering port of Las Palmas. Arriving at Tenerife on 19th May, one of the sailors was discharged due to sickness and, after spending twelve days unloading her cargo, the ship sailed southward to lift a cargo of grain in Argentina. By-passing Buenos Aires, the *Campus* crossed the bar at the island of Martin Garcia and, pushing hard against the current of the River Parana, steamed upriver to Rosario. The level of the river varied throughout the year and the river pilot had to contend with this. Captain Therbyson, aged sixty-one, had loaded grain numerous times at the various river ports and, although trusting the pilots to navigate, he was always alert to the dangers. Steamers coming downriver had a habit of suddenly sweeping unexpectedly from around bends, mud banks had a habit of shifting, but after twenty hours of river passage, the ship arrived at Rosario.

The *Campus* was a well-designed tramp and had four large cargo holds and an additional cross bunker hold, called no. 2A. This could store a large amount of coal and was divided from no. 2 cargo hold by a steel bulkhead. At Rosario all holds were partially filled with 4,280 tons of maize and the charterers, Louis Dreyfus & Co. who were the leading grain exporters in Argentina, required that the ship go back downriver and top off her cargo at the small port of Villa Constitucion and then sail for Hamburg. Captain Therbyson was not an expert in maize but he did know that if it was not dry it had the potential to heat and smoulder when compressed in a ship's hold – just like coal.

At Rosario a young Argentinian named Julian Petri was signed on as an ordinary seaman to replace the sick sailor left at Tenerife. It was Petri's first trip to sea. On 29th June with a pilot on board, the *Campus* sailed for Villa Constitucion which lay 33 miles downriver. The river above Villa Constitucion widens considerably and is divided into several channels, the view from a ship's bridge being one of numerous islands and channels looming up ahead. Down below in the engine-room the routine carried on as usual, watch followed watch as the regular throb of the engine drove the ship along. However, the routine of the engine-room was interrupted by the outbreak of a small fire in the port pocket bunker which contained about 3 tons of coal. Chief Engineer Victor Houston was not unduly concerned since these coals could be shovelled out into the stokehold and doused with water. This was done and the *Campus* tied up at the base of the cliffs at one of Villa Constitucion's two loading berths. Loading began in the afternoon with bulk maize flowing down chutes from warehouses higher up on the cliffs. Later in the day, a second small fire broke out amongst the coals in the port side of the cross bunker hold. This was dealt with similarly by raking out a ton of red-hot coals and hosing them down with river water.

The next day was Saturday and the Argentine stevedores would cease work at 1 pm for the weekend, but the morning session was enough to complete the loading and trim the cargo. Grain is a dangerous cargo because it moves around like water and one way to prevent it from shifting when a ship rolls is to place several layers of bagged grain on top. The ship's derricks were used to lift the heavy slings of bagged maize into the holds and, whilst this was going on, Captain Therbyson and Chief Engineer Houston went together to investigate the bunker spaces and see if outbreaks of fire were likely to recur. Satisfied, Captain

Therbyson noted in the ship's log book that all was in order. As noon passed, quietness descended over Villa Constitucion as the port stopped working and the rest of the town closed down for the afternoon siesta. However, the crew of the *Campus* still had work to do, covering the hatches and securing the derricks ready for sea. Captain Therbyson had received orders to sail as soon as possible for Las Palmas and Hamburg, and a pilot was even booked for Sunday to take the ship 160 miles downriver to the bar at Martin Garcia.

In those bygone days of ocean tramps, the River Plate was bustling with cargo ships. Invariably there was a hold-up at Martin Garcia as laden shipping waited for enough water to cross over the bar and out into the Plate estuary. Many a ship had scraped her bottom passing over rather than wait longer than was really necessary. 'Waiting for water' was a phrase that meant anchoring for perhaps a week until the signal station, perched on top of the huge granite mound known as the island of Martin Garcia, indicated that the level was up and ships could proceed. Straining at her anchor cable, the strong river current sweeping past, the crew of the *Campus* settled down to wait. On the bridge the officer of the watch continually kept an eye on other ships anchored nearby and frequently took bearings to check that his ship was not dragging her anchor. All tramp ship officers knew every granite block of the Martin Garcia signal station, which was also reputed to have some dark dungeons, as they had spent many hours studying it through their binoculars waiting for the signal to up anchor and cross the bar.

Two days passed when imperceptibly a smell of coffee – or was it roasting maize? – began to waft out of no. 2 hold. Captain Therbyson's suspicions were confirmed when the aroma became noticeably stronger and a puff of smoke began to curl out of a ventilator at the after end of the hold. Chief Engineer Houston went into the cross bunker hatch himself and discovered that there was indeed a fire deep down in the bunker. This time the seat of the fire could not be exposed and hoses were poked into the coals to give them a thorough drenching. Spontaneous combustion in bunker coal was known to cause the most obdurate of fires and a mass of white-hot coals buried under tons of other coal was notoriously difficult to extinguish. Worse still, heat was radiating from a white-hot patch of coals lying directly against the steel bulkhead which divided the bunker hold from the bone-dry maize in no. 2 hold. The bulkhead had heated and had slowly roasted the maize, hence the aroma of roasted coffee, until the maize had begun to smoulder and burn.

Captain Therbyson knew that the safety of the ship was at risk. With a fire in the bunkers and a hold of burning maize, he needed to reach a port which had fire-fighting capabilities such as Buenos Aires or Montevideo. The problem was that the *Campus* was bottled-up and unable to cross the bar for at least two more days! Counting the hours, the crew of the tramp ship toiled at hosing down the bunker coals and the maize. It was disheartening to see the maize simply soak up the water and continue to burn fiercely. Agonizingly they waited for the signal station to give them the all clear and other ships re-anchored to give the *Campus* a clear run out into the River Plate at the earliest opportunity. A pall of smoke hung over the ship and the smell of coffee turned into a peculiar combined stench of burning maize and coal. At long last the water over the bar was just enough for the *Campus* to escape and, with her windlass still heaving up the anchor, Captain Therbyson thrust the ship at full ahead.

Montevideo was chosen as the most suitable port to take in a burning steamer and the *Campus* made the 150-mile dash in record time. Sweeping into the outer harbour uniformed *bomberos* could be seen standing ready with hoses to fight the blaze. To eradicate all traces of fire, both holds had to be emptied. Lighters were brought alongside and, ton by ton, 2,400 tons of maize were lifted out of no. 2 hold. At the same time, 600 tons of bunker coal was landed on the quayside – a process which took five days The fire brigade swamped the coals with unending streams of water before being certain that all traces of fire had been extinguished. Burnt and tainted maize was dumped into the harbour but good maize was placed in the lighters for reloading. After eleven days, the wearisome task was completed and the *Campus,* none the worse for wear, sailed for Las Palmas and Hamburg.

Arriving at the German port, Julian Petri signed off with wages of £5. 7s. 5d. His first trip to sea had been an eventful one and he was last seen heading for the infamous Reeperbahn, the red light district of Hamburg. The Tempus Shipping Company, anticipating that Louis Dreyfus & Co. would not be pleased with the late delivery and loss of part of their cargo, prepared to face a legal dispute. Captain Therbyson was an experienced mariner whose business was commanding ships – legal problems were not his concern. He had done his duty and saved the ship and her cargo, although another day's delay at Martin Garcia and it might well have been a different story.

Chapter 11

The Valuable Persian Carpets

Ah Jong, the Chinese carpenter of the S.S. *Varsova* had a headache. The extreme heat of the Persian Gulf had made him feel unwell and on the morning of Sunday, 14th July 1929 he did not feel like doing his daily chore of sounding the bilges. Instead, and not for the first time, he guessed the measurements and wrote them into the chief officer's notebook.

The chief officer was Philip Savage, who had left his home in Suffolk to join the British India Steam Navigation Company in 1914. He had served with the company for fifteen years and was proud of his position with one of Britain's premier fleets. The BISN Co. had an impressive coat of arms which showed Britannia with the British lion carrying a shield emblazoned with the Union Jack. This well-known coat of arms was given to the company in recognition of its service in the South African war, and it had been given the privilege to use Britannia on its officers' cap badges and uniform buttons. British India ships were forever plying the eastern seas as they provided an essential regular cargo and passenger service that encompassed the Arabian Sea and the Bay of Bengal.

As a junior officer, Philip Savage had been appointed to the Bombay office. British India officers were either based at Bombay or Calcutta, the unwritten law of the company being that an officer spent his whole career based at the city where he had originally been appointed. The standard term of engagement was for two-and-a-half years, but it was not until the end of the war in 1918 that Philip Savage was able to take home leave. He remained with the company and achieved the rank of Chief Officer in 1923. He had spent many years gaining experience of handling a variety of cargoes and calling at Indian and Arabian ports, dealing with multitudes of Asiatic deck passengers.

British India ships had Indian crews and British officers, with the ship's carpenter invariably being Chinese. Orders were given in Hindustani and, after fifteen years service, Philip Savage could speak the language well. It was a chief officer's responsibility on any British ship to be in charge of the general maintenance of the ship and her deck equipment. During every voyage there is a constant need to prevent rust, keep the ship well-painted, and ensure all woodwork is sanded and varnished. A ship with a smart, clean appearance usually indicated an efficient chief officer and the BISN Co. demanded a very high standard from its officers. Undoubtedly Philip Savage was a very capable officer who could one day expect to be given his own command.

The daily routine at sea was designed to keep the ship spotless and a large Indian crew was carried for that purpose. The chief officer came on watch at 4 am, and Philip Savage liked to have the ship's decks thoroughly hosed and scrubbed before breakfast. For this purpose it was routine for the engine-room to have 'water on deck' at about that time every morning. The valve that supplied water for the deck hoses was located by no. 2 hatch and was turned on and off daily. However, there was another valve inside the hold that was kept closed, except to fight a fire, and it was protected by a large locked box. Chief Officer Savage was the keeper of the key and he kept it in his cabin.

The master of the *Varsova* was Richard Henry Power, an Irishman. He had held the BISN Co's rank of commander for four-and-a-half years. He had been up and down the Persian Gulf countless times, as the *Varsova* maintained a three-weekly schedule departing from Bombay and calling at miscellaneous ports including Karachi, Bandar Abbas, Bahrain, Kuwait, Mahomerah and Basra. The ship had four large cargo holds, accommodation for thirty first-class passengers, space for almost twelve hundred deck passengers and an important part of her service was to deliver mail on time. Swift passages were expected, and her engine-room was a powerhouse containing six main boilers driving twin screws and easily giving the ship a dashing speed of 15 knots. Captain Power needed a quick turnround at Basra and on Saturday, 13th July 1929 he was impatiently watching the last of the cargo disappearing into the holds. Looking out on the foredeck from the windows of his day cabin, he could see Chief Officer Savage peering intently into no. 2 hold. This was almost directly below his windows and it was obvious that the chief officer was preoccupied with something. The reason was that 390 bales of rare and exquisite Persian carpets were being loaded. It was by far the most valuable cargo for which Philip Savage had been responsible, and the merchants who were shipping the carpets trusted him to deliver them undamaged.

A knock on the solid teak door of his cabin roused Captain Power – his steward reminded him that he had an appointment. British India ships were

Despite many years' service with the British India Steam Navigation Co., Commander Power was dismissed for misconduct when a shipment of valuable carpets in the Varsova*'s hold was damaged by unknown persons.* Photograph courtesy of the World Ship Photo Library.

crewed by a unique system whereby an Indian *serang* (headman/bosun) of a ship would recruit a close-knit crew made up of relatives and fellow villagers. Problems among such a crew were traditionally dealt with by the *serang*, but sometimes petty feuds and jealousy needed to be sorted out by the commander. It was one of those rare occasions where Captain Power was obliged to discipline severely four of the Indian crew. He did this in a formal and fair manner, relying completely on the *serang*'s version of the complaint. In this case, Captain Power decided that the four seamen would be dismissed when the ship reached Bombay. Aggrieved, the four Indians plotted revenge and that night they crept into no. 2 hold. One of them slipped a well-greased arm between the water pipe and the locked box and maliciously eased the valve fully open.

It was after midnight when the *Varsova* left Basra for the return trip to Bombay. Basra lies surrounded by date palms at the head of the Shatt-el-Arab waterway and was known as the 'great date port of the world'. It was 50 miles from Basra to the open sea of the Persian Gulf and Captain Power was behind schedule. At 4.30 am the Shatt-el-Arab pilot was dropped and course was set for Bushire. At 5.00 am the *serang* as usual reported to the bridge for permission to start the daily five-hour ritual of hosing the decks. Chief Officer Savage routinely ordered water on deck from the engine-room and the pumping of water commenced immediately. However, not only did it gush from the deck hoses but, below and unseen, a fountain of sea water spurted out from the opened valve behind the locked box down in no. 2 hold. In the five hours that the pump was on, hundreds of tons of water had flooded into the lower hold, completely drowning the bales of Persian carpets. This happened during the morning when Ah Jong, the ship's carpenter, had his headache and failed to sound the bilges.

The *Varsova* anchored off Bushire at 1.30 in the extreme heat of the afternoon. Having been on the bridge for twelve hours, Captain Power left the ship in charge of Second Mate Brown and retired to his cabin. Whilst the ship was at anchor, it was one of the second mate's duties, as officer of the watch, to take the ship's draught fore and aft. By 2.45 pm he had the figures and he checked and checked them again. There was no doubt about it, the ship was unaccountably down by the head by 2 feet. He could just enter it in the log book and report it later but as the *Varsova* would shortly be underway, he felt that it was important enough to disturb Captain Power and tell him. He went down to the commander's cabin, where a slightly irritated captain listened to his concerns and merely said that he would have it checked again.

It was clear to Second Officer Brown that the commander did not take him seriously and therefore was not convinced that there was anything amiss. Nevertheless, he felt he ought to pursue the matter and after spending an uneasy half-an-hour decided to tell the chief officer. It was 3.40 pm and Chief Officer Savage was in his cabin taking tea before going up to the fo'c's'le to supervise the heaving up of the anchor. He listened patiently to Second Officer Brown's insistence that the ship was 2 feet down by the head and about Captain Power's disinterest. Philip Savage felt that the second officer had probably misread the draught, but as he seemed so insistent about it he sent Ah Jong to sound the forward bilges. Unknown to anybody, Ah Jong could not be bothered taking the soundings and falsely reported back that the bilges were dry.

At 4.17 pm the windlass was heaving the anchor cable short and a few minutes later the anchor broke the surface and was pulled up into the hawsepipe. Chief Officer Savage leaned far out over the rail to check that the anchor was securely home, and, as he did so, he casually looked at the white-painted numbers on the ship's bow. With some alarm he realized that Second Officer Brown had been right, the bow was a little low in the water. He turned to Ah Jong who was winding up the brakes on the windlass and brusquely asked him whether he had sounded the bilges.

The Chinaman's downcast eyes answered his question. Very much annoyed, the chief officer hurried up to the bridge and advised Captain Power of his discovery. Having genuinely sounded the bilges, Ah Jong now shamefacedly reported that there was 8 feet of water in no. 2 hold. With a sinking feeling, Philip Savage realized that the valuable Persian carpets were probably underwater, but Captain Power was more concerned that the ship had sprung a leak. The chief officer hurried to investigate, and the bilge pumps started to pump the water out. In the stuffy darkness of the hold, Chief Officer Savage surveyed the damage. To his dismay, the Persian carpets were awash with sea water, but where was the leak? Meticulously he used his powerful torch to look for clues. There were none.

Once the hold had been pumped dry, it stayed that way and the existence of a leak was discounted. The ship's officers were naturally at a loss to explain the inrush of water into the hold, and it was only as a last resort that the waterpipe was checked for a possible leak. The pipe itself was sound, but on unlocking the box it was seen that the valve was fully open – it had obviously been tampered with. Whoever had done the deed would reap a sweeter revenge than they could have hoped for.

In the teeming metropolis of Bombay, the quietness of the plush boardroom of the British India Steam Navigation Company was remarkable. The Board of Inquiry sat to find out why Commander Power had not acted promptly when warned of the vessel's draught by Second Officer Brown. They also wanted to know why Chief Officer Savage had allowed Ah Jong to become slack in his duties. In addition, the influential owners of the Persian carpets were very angry about the loss of their most valuable cargo, and the reputation of the company had suffered as a result.

In the event, the Board decided to terminate the employment of both Commander Power and Chief Officer Savage. After arriving in London and finding that the directors at the British India's head office in Leadenhall Street were unwilling to reconsider the decision, the two men turned to the courts to claim unfair dismissal. In March 1930 the judgement showed some sympathy for Captain Power, for his dismissal had been harsh, but the British India Company had firm legal grounds for doing so if they wished. As for Chief Officer Savage, his actions on board the *Varsova* that day did not, in the judge's view, warrant dismissal, and he was awarded twelve months salary with costs.

Chapter 12

Paradise on Earth

It was the first day of May 1903 and the heat in Calcutta was unbearable. Day after day the thermometer topped the century mark, and the atmosphere was oppressive. Ian Colvin, lately a journalist with the *Pioneer*, a Lahore newspaper, was travelling to South Africa to take up an appointment as assistant editor of the *Cape Times*. Although he knew India well, he disliked Calcutta immensely, and found himself stuck in a hotel with apathetic staff and abominable food. The days seemed endless as he waited to board the Natal Line steamer *Umona* to take him to Cape Town.

Finally, on 5th May, Ian Colvin made his way to the Natal Line's wharf and settled himself with great relief into a two-berth cabin on the *Umona*. Although the ship was registered in London, she was permanently employed on the Cape Town–Durban–Colombo–Calcutta run, and was manned by British officers and a lascar crew. There was accommodation for ten European passengers, but the ship was generally on charter to the Natal Emigration Department to carry Indian labourers, at £6 a head, to work in the sugar plantations of the Natal and Transvaal. In addition, the ship had loaded 1,470 tons of Indian cargo for Natal and Cape Town.

During the day, three other European passengers joined the ship. They were Mr. R.R. Martin, an American, Dr. Philipson, a South African and Mr. Simkins, a British tea planter from Assam. Also on board were Dr. Staunton, who was the surgeon-superintendent for the four hundred and seventy-five Indian men, women and children who were being taken to Natal. Assisting Dr. Staunton was Mr. McLaren, the 'chief compounder' for the Indians.

Ian Colvin found himself sharing a cabin with Christopher Simkins, the tea planter, and, both being adventurous characters in their twenties, they formed a friendship. On the morning of 6th May, the *Umona* left Garden Reach and headed down the turbid River Hooghly. The passengers had a small saloon and part of the afterdeck to themselves, while the multitude of Indian labourers and their families camped under wide awnings on the ship's foredeck. Soon a rising hubbub of voices and the penetrating odours of curry, rancid butter, Bombay duck, boiled rice and mutton cooked in coconut oil transformed the ship into a floating village. This domestic scene rapidly dispersed when the ship left the river and began to pitch into the waves of the Bay of Bengal making everybody seasick.

Captain Charles Hedley, master of the *Umona* for the past two years, had plied the route many times. It was a 28-day voyage from Calcutta to Durban and steaming southwards in the monsoon season was always a lively trip. Colombo was reached on 12th May and, as the ship was late due to bad weather, the captain was anxious to leave as soon as possible. The harbour pilot who took the *Umona* in stayed on board to take her out again, as five more European passengers hastily embarked for Durban. They had hardly been shown to their cabins when the ship was underway, the *Umona* impolitely cutting across the bows of an incoming passenger steamer. She cleared the limits of the harbour and steamed into the night.

That evening, dinner in the small saloon was a miserable affair and after introductions had been made, sea-sickness forced most of the passengers to retire to their cabins. All the new passengers were from Ceylon who were Mr. Siedle, his daughter and her friend Miss Robinson, Mr. Van Reenen, a Boer who had been held as a prisoner of war in Ceylon, and Mr. Mathewson, a tea planter.

Two days later strong headwinds, squalls and torrential rain slowed the progress of the *Umona* and Captain Hedley was faced with the unwelcome prospect of approaching the Maldive Islands in fading light. Ships sailing between the East and South Africa mostly used the deep and wide One and a Half Degree Channel to pass through the scattered atolls that make up the Maldives. Captain Hedley was quite sure of his latitude and longitude and decided to push on and pass through the channel, which was completely unmarked and unlit, that night. By this time most of the European passengers had found their sea legs and dinner in the saloon that evening was a convivial affair. From the bridge came the news that the ship was to pass through the Maldives that night and would be crossing the equator at about the same time the next day. Ian Colvin spent a relaxing evening in the cosy saloon, and it was just before midnight when he was the last passenger to turn in. He had been in his bunk for about three hours when the whole ship shook violently and the regular beat of the propeller abruptly stopped.

Shortly afterwards the Indian cabin steward rushed by crying out, "All passengers, you must get up!" The time was 2.45 am and the European passengers began to stumble out of their cabins, half-dressed and fumbling with their bulky life-jackets as they made their way out on deck. A full moon revealed a fairly calm sea, and from the foredeck came a loud jabbering of excited Indian voices. A line of white breakers could be made out and it was obvious that the ship had gone aground. For a brief moment the engines thundered astern, but then stopped. The lascar sailors began to swing the lifeboats out when a sudden fierce downpour of rain made the passengers scurry for the shelter of the saloon. In the dim darkness the situation seemed grim, there were hundreds of Indian deck passengers, yet the *Umona* carried only four lifeboats.

Fears were allayed when a number of palm-covered islands materialized in the early dawn. Thankfully one of them was within easy reach of the ship and would provide a refuge if need be. The tide was on the ebb and the ship was plainly stuck hard and fast by the bows, whilst at the stern no bottom was found when a 100-fathom deep-sea lead line was dropped over. The outgoing tide exposed a labyrinth of reefs and channels which offered an obstacle-studded pathway to the nearest island, perhaps 2 miles distant. The small jollyboat was lowered and after inspecting the hull for damage it was found that the ship was in no immediate danger. On the other hand, the forward two holds were leaking badly and the engine-room and stokehold bottom plates were pierced by sharp coral. The engine was undamaged and the pumps were set to work keeping the water level down. The steamer was safe for the moment but there was a danger that heavy seas would break her up or even sweep her away into deep water.

It was decided to land the hundreds of Indian men, women and children together with the nine European passengers. Mr. A.W. Bruckland, the chief officer and Mr. Siedle, who had some acquaintance with the Maldives and could speak a little Sinhalese and Hindustani, manned the jollyboat along with two lascar seamen. Ian Colvin jumped into the small boat so smartly that Captain Hedley did not object and the five men set off to explore the island. The glare of the morning sun was such that Ian Colvin was particularly pleased with the white solar topee that he had purchased in Calcutta – the Indian-made sun hats were not only a status symbol for Europeans in the East but also gave excellent protection against the hottest sun. The water proved too shallow for boat work, so the Indian seamen rowed back to the ship and Chief Officer Bruckland, Ian

Colvin and Mr. Siedle splashed and waded through the shallows until at last they plodded up the white sandy beach that encircled the island.

By chance, four Maldivians were gathering coconuts on what was otherwise an uninhabited island and Mr. Siedle was able to make them understand that the *Umona* was in trouble and that boats were needed. Although the Maldivians were surly and unwilling to help unless rewarded, they eventually loaded the coconuts in their canoe and set off for a large island in the distance. Left alone, the three men took stock of the situation. The island was covered in lush grass and bushes, wild flowers and pineapples were dotted amongst the countless coconut palms and there were a few large timber trees. The natural beauty of the place was not lost on them and they gazed at the vast vault of blue sky and the white clouds which tumbled above the wide horizon. Dark-purple waves broke on the outer reefs and these contrasted vividly with the tranquil turquoise water around the island. It was a paradise on earth

By the time they decided to return to the ship the tide had come in and they were stranded on the island. Ian Colvin was fascinated by the romantic picture that the *Umona* presented. The grey hull and white upperworks of the vessel stood out clearly against the background of a turquoise sea dotted with islands. Smoke drifted lazily out of her tall funnel and she appeared to be riding at anchor rather than trapped on a coral reef. Just then eight Maldivian sailing craft with large brown mat sails came up on the wind and swarmed around the *Umona*. It seemed that help had arrived to ferry the Indians from the ship to the island, so Captain Hedley sent the jollyboat over to bring back his chief officer, along with Ian Colvin and Mr. Siedle.

The visit by the Maldivians had not been pleasant. Their intention had been to loot the ship but they were frightened off when Captain Hedley threatened them with a large revolver. Instead, they resorted to demanding sacks of rice before they would do anything to help. The British officers were uneasy about the lack of hospitality shown by these particular people and decided to forego their help. Arrangements were made to start landing all the passengers by walking ashore at low tide the following morning. Night fell and the nervous murmurings of almost five hundred people who longed to be on dry land gradually faded away until only the sound of the ocean filled the night. Occasionally the ship grated on the coral and lurched to seaward and the possibility that she might slip off the reef and sink in deep water became a major concern.

Captain Hedley had no intention of leaving his ship, but it was essential to evacuate the Indian migrants and European passengers. Early next morning the gangway was fully lowered and a hundred Indian men, each carrying a bundle of possessions and a canister of water, were guided by Chief Officer Bruckland as they slithered and stumbled over rocks and waded through pools to the island. Once there, they started clearing a campsite and making huts of plaited palm leaves under the direction of Mr. McLaren and Dr. Staunton. Hovering in the background, the Maldvians watched as the tide rose. After another round of haggling and offers of a great deal of rice, they were persuaded to use their sailing craft to land the remaining three hundred and seventy-five Indians. By that evening, the evacuation had been successfully completed and Captain Hedley turned his attention to sending a message to Colombo that a large number of castaways needed to be rescued.

The *Umona* had actually run aground on the north edge of the well-known Suvadiva Atoll, which lies on the south side of the One and a Half Degree Channel. Celestial observations confirmed that the ship was 76 miles off her course having been gripped by a strong current over a period of just twelve hours. The *Umona* carried ample provisions to feed the castaways but since passing steamers would keep to the centre of the channel, it was doubtful if the wreck would be noticed. It was therefore decided to sail a ship's lifeboat directly to Colombo to seek help – 480 miles away.

The familiar grey hulls of the Bullard King's Natal Line were a feature of South African ports. The Umona *ran aground in the Maldive Islands whilst bringing many field labourers from Calcutta to work in the sugar plantations of Natal and became a total loss.* Photograph courtesy of the Martin Leendertz Collection, Ship Society of South Africa.

Chief Officer Bruckland was confident that with the south-west monsoon winds behind him he could sail to the coast of Ceylon in only five days. From the many who volunteered to go with him, Captain Hedley chose Third Officer Tollemache, Ian Colvin and Chris Simkins. The ship's *serang* (bosun) and a lascar seaman completed the crew. As conditions were perfect no time was wasted and a lifeboat – a wooden, double-ended boat about 26 feet long and capable of being rowed or sailed – was prepared straight away. That evening casks of water and tins of bully beef, ship's biscuits and condensed milk were put on board, along with a tarpaulin, a medicine chest, an oilbag and a sea anchor. To be able to navigate accurately, Chief Officer Bruckland took with him a compass, a chart and his own sextant and pocket watch. Captain Hedley and the remaining officers wished them godspeed and the six men dropped down into the waiting lifeboat and, with a last farewell, sailed off into the night.

Soon afterwards the wind began to blow in fierce squalls and, with the sail lowered, the lifeboat ran before the wind. It was a wild ride and although seasick, cold and wet, the men bailed for their lives. It was only by streaming the sea anchor and oil bag (letting them out on a line to calm the sea) that the boat stayed upright. Lost in a world of mountainous waves and shrieking winds it took a superhuman effort from Chief Officer Bruckland and Third Officer Tollemache, who took turns at the tiller and managed to keep the boat from capsizing. Finally after three days the storm blew itself out, the weather improved and they were able to set a course for Colombo harbour.

Their next affliction was the terrific heat in the afternoons, made worse because their sun hats had either been washed overboard or reduced to a soggy pulp. To provide a sleeping place, two planks were lashed lengthways across the thwarts and over this an awning was rigged using an oar and the tarpaulin. Inside this tent it was as hot as an oven, but at least it was out of the direct heat of the sun's rays. At noon on the fourth day Chief Officer Bruckland obtained a perfect noon sight of the sun, from which he worked out that they had barely covered 60 miles and had been blown dangerously southwards. The prospect of missing Ceylon altogether and ending up in the Bay of Bengal was an unwelcome thought. The lifeboat was steered towards the north, a gentle south-westerly breeze helping them on their way. At this point, Chief Officer Bruckland became ill with heat stroke and navigation became the responsibility of Third Officer Tollemache. Progress was good and for day after day the lifeboat sailed northwards until on the eighth day they had reached the latitude of Colombo, when an easterly course was steered in the expectation of making a landfall. Great was the excitement the following morning when not only did the coast appear ahead of them, but also the unmistakeable outline of Adam's Peak, which meant that they were bearing straight down on Colombo Harbour! After spending a long afternoon sailing in, a stiff pull on the oars took them through the entrance between the two great breakwaters and they slipped into the harbour unnoticed. It was evening but there was light enough for them to make out the imposing shape of a British cruiser among the steamers lying at their mooring buoys. They rowed up to HMS *Pique*, were taken on board and their mission was complete.

The *Umona* was abandoned and all the castaways were rescued. Chief Officer Bruckland and Third Officer Tollemache were awarded the Lloyd's Silver Medal for Meritorious Service in recognition of their bravery.

Chapter 13

Hardship on Gardner Island

Second Mate Henry Cleveland Lott, fresh from a week's home leave, took the train from his home in Folkestone to rejoin his ship at Immingham on the north-east coast of England. The year was 1929 and the S.S. *Norwich City* had been chartered, along with many other British tramp ships, to carry coal to Australia where strikes had disrupted supplies to power stations. The 18-year-old ship was owned by the Reardon Smith Line and was fitted with oil tanks as well as coal bunkers to provide fuel for her boilers. The vessel was a typical tramp ship, of nondescript appearance, with four cargo holds and a cross bunker hatch between the bridge deck and the tall smoke stack. She also had accommodation for thirty-five officers and crew.

It was an uneventful trip to Australia and after completing discharge at Melbourne, the ship sailed for Vancouver on 17th November. The freighter was in ballast and 'flying light' easily averaged 10 knots towards Honolulu where it had been arranged she would take on bunkers. Her master was Captain Daniel Hamer, aged thirty-eight, who came from Barry in Wales. He had obtained his first command in 1922, and had joined the well-known Reardon Smith Line in 1926. He had been master of the *Norwich City* for only seven months but was quite used to life on board tramp ships, where voyages around the world could last for up to two years. On this trip they expected to be spending a wintry Christmas in Vancouver.

After passing north-west of the Fiji Islands, the ship encountered cyclonic disturbances that lasted for several days. Strong gales, rough seas and heavy rain hurled the ship around and set her badly off course. Overcast skies made celestial observations impossible and, with no land in sight, there was no way of establishing the vessel's position. By Friday, 29th November Captain Hamer was navigating by dead reckoning which at best could be described as educated guesswork. He called Chief Officer Thomas and Second Mate Henry Lott to the chartroom and jointly they concluded that the ship was far from any land. The closest land to them was the low-lying Phoenix Islands, but the three experienced navigators were confident that the *Norwich City* was well clear of that island group.

That evening Henry Lott was drowsing on the settee in his cabin and at midnight he was due to take over as officer of the watch from Third Mate Caldcleugh. The monotonous thumping of the engine and the ceaseless motion of the ship made sleep difficult, but he needed to rest. Suddenly, he stiffened involuntarily as he felt, rather than heard, an almighty crash. The ship quivered, the engine-room telegraph jangled and the *Norwich City* shuddered to a dead stop. Lott looked at his watch, it was 11.05 pm. He grabbed his jacket and made his way up to the bridge. The wind was howling and a white foam smothered the forepart of the ship. Neither Captain Hamer nor anybody else had any idea where they were but the ship had obviously driven hard onto a reef. All hands were told to put their life jackets on and Chief Officer Thomas and the carpenter spent a precarious half-an-hour sounding the bilges to confirm the damage. Meanwhile, Captain Hamer mustered the crew outside the galley where they were best sheltered from the blasting wind and drenching spray. Apart from the cacophony of the sea, the relentless echoing from the empty holds as the keel grated on the reef was the most ominous sound. It was after midnight and Henry Lott knew that the seas were too rough to launch a lifeboat. Whatever happened they would have to stay put until the morning. The captain deduced that they were probably on uninhabited Gardner Island, one of the far-flung Phoenix Group, 1,800 miles south-west of the Hawaiian Islands and 600 miles north of Samoa. Wireless Operator Clark, ensconced in his small radio shack behind the wheelhouse, began to transmit a distress call giving their position, and this was eventually picked up and acknowledged by Apia Radio Station in Samoa.

The strain on the vessel's hull was tremendous as the waves remorselessly smashed against the reef and swirled around the trapped ship. Inevitably the ship's double bottom oil fuel tanks ruptured and the leaking oil reached the hot furnaces and burst into flames. It was 4 am when Captain Hamer addressed the crew who huddled around him to catch every word. With the fire taking hold in the engine-room, it was Captain Hamer's decision that they must abandon ship. The crew was reluctant because the boatdeck was high above the sea and, in the darkness, few were keen to risk their lives in the churning sea below. Setting an example, Captain Hamer supervised the swinging out of the port lifeboat and, as he did so, a series of heavy seas swept the *Norwich City* making her shudder violently. An immense wave wrenched the lifeboat from its davits and, before anyone realized it, Captain Hamer had been swept away. Chief Officer Thomas seized the initiative and, knowing that the one remaining wooden lifeboat was in danger of being destroyed by the intense fire that was burning below, got all hands over to the starboard lifeboat. It was his intention to lower this boat until it was level with the main deck where it could be boarded and lowered quickly if necessary. Hopefully, it would then be possible to remain on the ship until morning, or even longer if the sea did not calm down.

The sun's rays began to illuminate a wild dawn and the crew were surprised to see how close the rocky shore was to the ship's starboard side. Tea was brewed in the galley and the cook and the galley boy began preparing welcome hot food. The oil-fed fire in the engine-room was roaring out of control and everybody knew it was only a matter of time before they would have to abandon ship or risk being burnt to death. Several loud explosions followed by flames bursting up out of the engine-room skylight meant that the time had come sooner than expected. Chief Officer Thomas promptly ordered all thirty-four hands, plus the ship's dog, to take their places in the lifeboat. The men crowded into the boat and it began to be lowered jerkily, using the oars to fend her off the ship's side. Hitting the water when the falls (the ropes holding the lifeboat to the davits) were released, the boat smacked into the swirling water. For a moment all seemed well, but a surging wave corkscrewed the boat around and capsized it, throwing everyone into the sea.

Henry Lott found himself cast into the sea but managed to grab one of the dangling manila rope falls. The sea flung him hard against the ship's side and he let go the rope, was sucked under and washed ashore. Half-drowned, he staggered along the stony beach conscious of other bedraggled figures around him. One particular figure looked familiar and he was astonished to see Captain Hamer, who had somehow survived being washed overboard.

In the blustery conditions the beach was a cold place, and the survivors gathered around the upturned starboard lifeboat which had been washed ashore. Trapped underneath were four crew and the ship's dog, who were quickly released, although one man had drowned. Captain Hamer listed the eleven crew who had not survived – six Arab firemen, the third and fourth engineers, the carpenter, a steward and a seaman. The twenty-four survivors stood together, grateful to be alive. Although they were cold and wet their attention was fixed on the *Norwich City* – her bow was high up on a reef and most of her hull was exposed to view as the tide receded. Smoke and flames had turned the ship into a blazing funeral pyre and it made an impressive, never-to-be-forgotten sight.

With such a dramatic backdrop it was some time before they realized that their landing place was an inhospitable, windswept spot being constantly bombarded by booming surf. All hands began making a tent out of the lifeboat's sails and, when the port lifeboat was discovered washed up on the beach, they spent the day carrying the few extra provisions and gear to the tent. With everything damp, it was only with difficulty that a fire was lit and a meeting held. Wireless Operator Clark confirmed that his SOS call had been acknowledged and Captain Hamer told the men to keep their spirits up because help was on the way. Their mood was cheerful as they settled down for the night, but sleep eluded them when the island's wildlife found their camp irresistible and crabs, ants, spiders and rats literally swarmed in, under and over the tent.

From behind Beach Road, the township of Apia fronted the exquisite harbour. According to the locals, the only thing spoiling the view was the rusting wreck of the German battleship *Adler* quietly disintegrating on a reef after being caught in the terrific hurricane of 1889. Captain J.H. Swindale, master of the British tramp *Trongate* of London, was surprised to receive an urgent invitation to go to Government House to meet with His Excellency the Administrator of Western Samoa. Once there, he was formally requested to take a surf boat and native crew on board his ship and to sail forthwith for Gardner Island to render assistance to the shipwrecked crew of the *Norwich City*. The Government guaranteed that the expenses of the rescue would be met, and by 2 o'clock on Saturday, 30th November the *Trongate* had steam up and was heading northwards towards the islands.

Gardner Island is surrounded by a fringe of reefs which dry out at low water. As is usual with small Pacific islands, the ocean around them is extremely deep and ships cannot anchor offshore. To land on such islands, it was the practice for a ship to drift off the island and send in a surf boat. On the morning of 3rd December the castaways on Gardner Island were delighted as not one, but two ships appeared on the horizon. The burnt-out wreck of the *Norwich City* was the most conspicuous object on the island and as the castaways had spent days building a huge bonfire to make doubly sure that they were seen, it was set on fire.

One ship was the *Trongate* and the other was a Norwegian oil tanker, the *Lincoln Ellsworth,* which had responded independently to the SOS. Captain Swindale, an old Pacific hand, took his steamer in close and the surf boat was lowered into the water. Crewed by six powerful islanders, the surf boat skilfully negotiated the curling ocean combers and landed close to the wreck of the freighter. The islanders heaved their surf boat well clear of the breakers and were warmly welcomed by the castaways. Rescue was not going to be easy as the seas were gigantic and the coral reefs offered no safe landing place. Sharks had been seen and, in fact, it was later learnt that the locality was renowned and feared for its sharks. The native crew set off to search for a better landing place and after a while they chose a location about a mile and a half away. The surf boat was lifted and carried by all hands and taken to a spot where there was a gap in the coral. By mid-afternoon the islanders announced that conditions were good and that they were ready to return to the *Trongate*. The surf boat had room for only three passengers and Captain Hamer asked for volunteers. Without enthusiasm, the wireless operator, the cook and the cabin boy elected to go first. The noise of the surf was deafening and attempting to cross it in a fragile surf boat was not an inviting prospect, but having crouched down in the bottom of the boat there was no time to be afraid. Once through the curling rollers, the natives paddled for all they were worth until they reached the relatively calm deep water. A long blast from the *Trongate's* fog horn greeted this success.

On the morning of the fourth day and after another unpleasant night, each man prepared to leave the island and take the wild ride in the surf boat. To speed up operations the Norwegian tanker came in closer and sent her motor launch to meet the surf boat and take off the men after each rescue. Captain Hamer was the last to leave and went on board the modern Norwegian vessel with half of his crew. Second Mate Henry Lott found himself on the *Trongate* along with eleven other crew members. It had been the bravery of the islanders that had made the rescue possible and the Administration of Western Samoa recognized this by awarding them £5 each with a recommendation for a Lloyd's Life Saving Medal. Captain Swindale of the *Trongate* received an official letter expressing appreciation for his prompt departure from Apia and for the manner in which he conducted the rescue.

When Captain Hamer arrived in Sydney, he found that the newspapers had been reporting the story of the shipwreck and rescue in full and were anxious to interview him. Although he was reticent, he allowed Apprentice T.G. Stephenson to give a description of the reality of being a castaway on a desert island.

'Our chief difficulty was to find water. We discovered one small hole, but it very soon dried up, and I doubt if we could have lived long had the rescue ships not arrived as they did.

It was a most desolate island, consisting chiefly of coral and sand, and although there was a limited supply of coconuts and sea birds were easy to catch, we were glad to see the last of it'.

The Sydney Morning Herald, 17th December 1929.

Chapter 14

The Seventy-Third Time

Originating in the days of sail, the Brocklebank Line was one of the oldest shipping companies in the world. Its elegant fleet came to be synonymous with the Liverpool–Calcutta trade and the company was noted for its tradition of naming ships with Asiatic names beginning with 'Ma'. For its part in rescuing British refugees in the Indian Mutiny of 1857, the company was granted the unique right to fly its blue and white house flag from the foremast. In fact, the story goes that the blue and white 'A' flag of the International Code of Signals was deliberately designed as a swallow-tailed flag in deference to the famous Brocklebank house flag.

A distinctive white band around the black hulls of the steamers recalled the days when the gun ports of sailing ships were painted white, and indeed the first Brocklebank ship of 1770 carried eighteen guns. Crews engaged on Brocklebankers understood that:

'Any member of the crew using obscene or profane language or is guilty of improper conduct, will forfeit two days pay'.

Ship's articles, S.S. *Maimyo.*

The requirement for the sailors to wear company uniform and the expectation of high standards of behaviour made the Line similar to the Royal Navy in some respects.

William Davies joined this prestigious company as an apprentice and, by 1918, he had attained the rank of chief officer with an extra master's certificate. Nevertheless, it was only after many years as a chief officer that he was given his first command in September 1934. He then spent eighteen months as a relieving master around the British coast before he was permanently appointed to the *Maimyo*. He knew the ship well because he had once been her chief officer. On 4th November 1936 the *Maimyo* sailed from the Brocklebank Dock in Liverpool direct for Calcutta, a port that Captain Davies had visited seventy-two times previously during his career.

> 'He had great experience of this coast, having as First Officer and as Master done about 72 journeys along that particular route.'
>
> The Times of Ceylon, *13th January 1937.*

Arriving at Calcutta on 9th December, the ship was efficiently unloaded and then fully loaded with bales of jute, chests of tea, gunnies, shellac, rice and dahl during a hectic nine days. The abdication of Edward VIII was the main topic of conversation, and by the time the ship left for London via Colombo at 11.30 am on the 18th the Empire had a new king. Dropping the Hooghly pilot, departure was taken from Sand Heads and, as was the custom, the ship was set on a course of S 23° W (true) until sighting the east coast of Ceylon.

The S.S. Maimyo. Photograph courtesy of the National Maritime Museum, London.

Both Captain Davies and Chief Officer Scions had spent years navigating ships between Calcutta and Colombo and both harbours were like second homes to them. They knew the *Bay of Bengal Pilot* manual by heart, which particularly warned mariners of the dangerous nature of the east coast of Ceylon. Landmarks and lighthouses were virtually non-existent on some sections of the coast and it was common knowledge that over the years several steamers had become stranded because of abnormal currents and hazy conditions.

Well aware of this, Captain Davies confidently expected to make his favourite landfall of the mountains behind the Komari Reef from a distance of 10 miles during the mid-morning of 24th December. The coastline of Ceylon at this point is made up of a large number of reefs and rocks that run out for almost 2 miles to form the dangerous Komari Reef. The usual route for steamers coming from Calcutta, Rangoon or Madras to Colombo was to make their landfall on this part of the coast, because once the mountain peaks were in distant view, course could be altered to keep well clear of the reef, pass the Basses Ridges and then round Dondra Head to Colombo.

Four days after clearing Sand Heads, noon sights taken on 23rd December showed that the *Maimyo* was on course, but when clouds covered the sky for the rest of the day no further observations could be taken. The distance of the ship from land was calculated to be 107 miles at 3.23 pm and 83 miles at twilight, and by the time Second Officer Allan came on watch at midnight the nearest land was reckoned to be 35 miles away. Although the ship's position had not been verified for twelve hours he knew they were well outside the 100-fathom line and would be in deep water for several hours yet. Weary after so long on the bridge, Captain Davies retired to his cabin to snatch a few hours rest, with orders to call him when the expected mountains were in sight. By 3.45 am the tropical dawn was breaking and Second Officer Allan was nearing the end of his watch. Up ahead and away on the starboard bow lay the coast of Ceylon, although it was not yet visible. There was a gentle breeze with an easy swell as the *Maimyo* pushed through the sea at 10½ knots and the day promised to be clear for navigating the ship around the Basses and Donra Head to Colombo. The half-light was now good enough for him to notice a dark shape on the horizon, and, as it was roughly where land might be sighted, he studied it through his powerful binoculars.

Punctual as ever, Chief Officer Scions came onto the bridge at precisely 3.55 am for the change of watch. Second Officer Allan quickly pointed out what he had seen and together the two experienced officers debated if it was land or not. According to the ship's dead reckoning, land should not be in sight for at least another two hours. Chief Officer Scions decided to call the captain who arrived in his pyjamas to join his officers. Since it was now officially the chief officer's watch, it was Mr. Scions who later made the entry in the log book.

'Light wind sea and swell. Clear cloudy weather. 4 am called Capt
to investigate dark shadow on the horizon. We directed our
binoculars on to it and felt confident that it was a cloud.
Official Log, S.S. Maimyo, *24th December 1936*

For a long time the three pairs of binoculars remained focused on the horizon. There were no sign of breakers to indicate land and with their combined years of navigating in eastern waters they concluded that it was a cloud, and the *Maimyo* held her course. Captain Davies announced that he was going to wash and dress before returning to the bridge for another look. He had just reached his cabin when, with a fearful crash, the ship jolted and smashed her way across a barrier of rock. Captain Davies rushed back to the bridge to met by a dumbfounded Chief Officer Scions. The light had played a devilish trick. The distant 'shadow' was, in fact, the mountain range they sought and the shoreline was less than a third of a mile away! The official log book only hints at the anguish of Captain Davies as he struggled to get his ship off the reef.

'Engines were stopped. 4.18 Full astern. 4.22 Stop.
4.24 Full astern. 4.38 Stopped engines.
4.40 Full astern. 5.38 Stop. 6.18 Full astern.
6.28 Stop. 7.00 Full astern. 7.04 Stop.
We desisted in trying to get the vessel off owing
to heavy water in forward holds.'

The *Maimyo* was on an even keel and stuck fast. The sea was a nest of reefs and in the sparkling reflection of the sunlight they could make out dark patches of rocks around them. Sea water rapidly filled the forepeak and no. 1 hold to a depth of 24 feet, which showed that the ship had actually come to grief on a well-submerged part of the reef. The pumps were concentrated on the rising level of water in no. 2 hold and, giving his position as latitude 7°05' N, longitude 81°52' E, (3 miles north of the Komari Reef), Captain Davies sent out an urgent call for assistance to Colombo.

Apart from the thump of the pumps, the ship was strangely silent, the only noise made by hordes of shrieking seagulls as they circled above. Since the weather was fine and the sea calm, refloating seemed a distinct possibility. Radio messages flew between the *Maimyo* and Colombo resulting in the Government salvage tug *Hercules* being despatched and due to arrive within twenty-four hours. Without knowing the true extent of the underwater damage, Captain Davies was advised to wait for the arrival of the professional salvors before making any further attempts to to move the ship.

Christmas Day began with a light breeze and gentle swell. The water in no. 2 hold had gained on the pumps and was now at 15 feet, so great was the relief when the *Hercules* hove into view at 11 am. Owing to the rocks in the vicinity of the *Maimyo*, the tug did not come alongside but anchored some way off. The rest of the day was spent waiting while two divers painstakingly examined the ship's bottom. They reported that the steel plating was ripped from the stem to the bridge and the ship's after section was resting firmly on a ridge of rock. The tug skipper's opinion was that all cargo had to jettisoned before any attempt at pulling the steamer off the rocks could be attempted.

The Brocklebank Line's agents in Colombo kept the head office in Liverpool informed of the situation. It was taken for granted that all water-damaged cargo would be jettisoned but cargo from the afterholds could be salvaged, and on 26th December the following cable was despatched to the agents.

> 'In our opinion lightening should begin forthwith. All available
> lighters should be secured and despatched to the ship without
> delay with necessary labour.'
>
> *Lloyds Weekly Casualty Reports,* 1st January 1937

Meanwhile the British India Steam Navigation Company's coastal steamer *Chantala,* which happened to be in Colombo Harbour, was promptly chartered to tow four large lighters out to the *Maimyo*. These were plentiful in Colombo, as all ships were loaded and unloaded as they lay between mooring buoys. Accordingly Captain Davies put the crew to work emptying no. 1 hold. Even using the ship's derricks it was still a back-breaking task to hook the sodden and expanded bales of gunnies and dump them over the side. Good cargo was stacked on deck ready for the lighters but progress was painfully slow.

Although the *Maimyo* was in the midst of a jumble of rocks, there was clear water at her stern to a depth of 40 feet. This promised an escape route, if only she could be pulled clear of the rocks then her own power could be used to claw her way free. The main difficulty was the 9,000 tons of cargo and the weight of sea water in her forward holds. The overall feeling was that the ship was doomed, especially when *Hercules* was ordered back to Colombo for pressing harbour duties. The jettisoning continued but signs of the tremendous strain on the hull and superstructure began to appear. On 29th December the weather changed and heavy swells swept over the decks and the hatches had to be battened down. Inevitably water found its way into no. 3 and no. 4 holds and it became a race against time to salvage any cargo at all.

On New Year's Day, *Chantala* arrived towing the four large lighters and anchored as close as she dared. The lighters were manoeuvred alongside *Maimyo* and more than a hundred Colombo labourers swarmed on board. They set to with a will and, by midnight, 200 tons of valuable cargo had been discharged, with only heavy rain putting a stop to their toil.

Wearily, Captain Davies entered his cabin and after taking off his wet clothes he lay down exhausted. It had been nine long days and nights of unending problems and dashed hopes since the ship had grounded and he had hardly slept. Dozing off, he was rudely awakened by Chief Officer Scions – it was 2 am and the news was bad. Sea water was rapidly filling no. 3 hold and even spurting through the steel bulkhead into the engine-room. Captain Davies ordered that the pumps be switched from no. 2 to no. 3 hold, but this did little to improve matters and the bulkhead was found to be bulging from the pressure of water against it. During the morning as cargo continued to be salvaged, the bulkhead collapsed and water cascaded into the engine-room. In the space of an hour the cylinder tops were underwater and the engine-room was abandoned. It was the beginning of the end, and three days later Captain Davies formally abandoned the ship. She sat on the bottom, her entire hull awash in 25 feet of water.

The Court of Inquiry into the loss of the *Maimyo* was held in Colombo and on Monday 11th January, immaculately dressed in white uniforms and solar topees, Captain Davies, Chief Officer Scions and Second Officer Allan made their way from their hotel to the District Court. The Inquiry was to determine if the ship had been lost by unavoidable causes or if the loss was due to a wrongful act by the master, the first officer or the second officer. All three men were well-represented by counsel and they were aware that their future careers were at stake.

It was quickly established that there was no charge for Chief Officer Scions to answer and the following day it was apparent that Second Officer Allan was blameless. The evidence against Captain Davies suggested that the stranding was not due to unavoidable circumstances since it could have been prevented by taking soundings. However, due to his long experience of navigating the coast, it was accepted that he had steered the same course and made the same allowances for currents so many times that he had no reason to stop the ship and take soundings. The Inquiry concluded that an abnormal current had pushed the *Maimyo* off her course, and took into consideration the fact that a freak trick of the light had deceived the three experienced officers. In view of this, Captain Davies' master's certificate was returned to him without cancellation or suspension. However, the court offered a word of advice to Captain Davies, it being that in future he should pay greater attention to the *Bay of Bengal Pilot* and to the warnings given on Admiralty chart 813 of the east coast of Ceylon.

The *Maimyo* was a familiar vessel in those waters, and for the many ships' officers who knew her the circumstances that led to her loss were a mystery. The *Maimyo* did not fade from memory for she became a feature of the coast for many years and an additional entry was included in the *Pilot*.

'The wreck of the *S.S. Maimyo*, with masts, funnel and upperworks showing, was, in 1938 situated close inshore northward of Sangama Kanda Point.'

Bay of Bengal Pilot, 1940.

Chapter 15

Nearly on the Green

The 'Ships movements and news' page of the Cape Town newspaper *Cape Argus* of Wednesday, 15th December 1937 informed readers that the *Stuart Star* had left harbour bound for Port Elizabeth and East London the day before. Readers were also informed that the passenger liner *Dunbar Castle* would be leaving for England at daybreak on Christmas Day. There was no connection between these announcements, but it was just a few days later that hasty preparations were being made on board the *Dunbar Castle* to accommodate a number of unexpected passengers. They were British seamen, most of the crew of the *Stuart Star*, which had been wrecked off the harbour approaches to East London.

At the seaside resort of East London, it was the beginning of the Christmas holiday season. Overlooking the balmy Indian Ocean was the East London Golf Club, but on the morning of 17th December play had been delayed due to patchy sea fog swirling over the course. Heavy fogs are a characteristic of this part of the South African coast but as the sun warms the day they usually clear away. As members waited in the clubhouse they could hear a faint blaring of ships' sirens and tugs' whistles as the Union Castle liner, *Balmoral Castle*, on time as usual, was in the process of entering Buffalo Harbour. The golf course extended down to beyond Hood Point where a lighthouse stood warning shipping to keep clear of the rocky shore. At about 10.30 am the fog began to lift and the golfers prepared to start their rounds. Emerging from the clubhouse they received word that a British cargo ship was aground not far from the eighteenth green. This news postponed play for the day, as in no time at all the course was invaded by hundreds of unwelcome spectators, all anxious to get a close-up view of the stranded ship.

The *Stuart Star* had left Liverpool on 20th November 1937 bound for South African and Australian ports. Having called at Cape Town and Port Elizabeth, the ship still had 520 tons of cargo for East London, 1,100 tons for Durban and 280 tons for Lourenço Marques. She left Port Elizabeth in the evening to make the short passage of 140 miles to East London, intending to arrive in the morning. A blanket of sea fog covered the coast but, in the murky night, the powerful light on Bird Island was picked up enabling the *Stuart Star* to proceed at full speed towards her destination. The large freighter was usually employed by the Blue Star Line on the United Kingdom–Argentina run and, being a fully refrigerated ship, she was used mainly to bring frozen meat from Uruguay and Argentina to England. Her master, Captain James Sinclair, had been with the company for many years and had spent most of his time at sea in and out of River Plate ports. He was a vastly experienced navigator and had spent the whole night on the bridge as he was wary of the notoriously rugged and often fog-bound South African coast.

Captain Sinclair imagined that by the time his ship reached the approaches to East London visibility would be clear. The entrance to Buffalo Harbour was narrow and not easy to negotiate even in fine weather. Added to this was the fact that because the harbour opens straight into the Indian Ocean the water is so deep that it is impracticable to drop anchor. If, on arrival, the fog still persisted, Captain Sinclair intended to station extra lookouts and slowly drift a mile or so off the entrance, sounding the fog horn until the fog lifted. He knew that although there was a lighthouse on Hood Point, there was strangely no shore-based fog horn to help ships when they most needed it.

At 5 am, Great Fish Point Lighthouse was estimated to be 6 miles off the port beam, which gave an estimated time of arrival at East London of 9 am. An hour later, Wireless Operator Hammond was doing his best to pick up a radio bearing from the East London signal station. For some reason he was unable to get a single bearing, although he was convinced that the radio direction-finding equipment was not faulty. However, he was able to make voice contact with the port authorities and told Captain Sinclair that the *Balmoral Castle* was up ahead and would shortly be entering harbour. Captain Sinclair raised his bushy eyebrows at this, for it seemed to him that the fog was too dense for a ship to enter harbour safely. In fact, the busy East London pilots had evolved a method for berthing ships in fog. They would station a tug across the harbour entrance continuously blowing her whistle, and this signal would give the pilot of an incoming ship enough sense of direction to allow him to take his charge into harbour.

It was now after 8 am, very foggy, and somewhere close ahead was East London. Captain Sinclair stopped the ship and called Chief Officer Edgar Rhodes to assist him on the bridge because he was perplexed by the odd series of blasts and hoots coming out of the fog. Edgar Rhodes had been chief officer of the *Stuart Star* since her maiden voyage ten years previously and, like Captain Sinclair, his experience was of mainly South American ports. Together they discussed the best way to approach the harbour when a clear patch appeared in the fog which revealed the harbour breakwater some distance away. A relieved Captain Sinclair considered that his ship was in no danger and allowed the chief officer to leave the bridge and take his station on the fo'c's'le head. He anticipated that the harbour pilot had seen them and was on his way.

Meanwhile, fog or no fog, the chief pilot of East London was berthing the *Balmoral Castle.* A second pilot was waiting in the launch at the end of the breakwater to go out to the *Stuart Star* as soon as the grey, clammy fog thinned. However, a sudden increase in the thickness of the fog surprised the pilot and he delayed his departure for a while. Captain Sinclair was also surprised as the fog came down again and he set the engines to slow ahead, hopefully to pick up the pilot. By 9.40 am the fog was as thick as ever and Captain Sinclair was resigned to spending the rest of the morning waiting for conditions to improve. Peering through his binoculars for the umpteenth time, he caught a momentary glimpse

Firmly on the rocks adjacent to the East London Golf Course and the Hood Point Lighthouse, the wreck of the Stuart Star *became a well-known landmark.*Photograph courtesy of Cape Independent Newspapers.

of breakers on the port bow. His nerves jangled as some sixth sense warned him that danger was perilously close

He snapped out an order for full ahead, and followed it up with an order to the quartermaster to ease the wheel hard over to starboard. It was too late. The port side of the ship crunched heavily against a rocky outcrop. Captain Sinclair quietly told the fourth officer to put the engine to full astern and waited for what seemed like an eternity for the ship to move. After seven minutes of racing the twin screws in reverse, it was obvious that the ship was stuck fast and a grim-faced James Sinclair ordered the engines to be stopped.

Second Officer Cummings was in his cabin prior to taking station aft for docking, when he felt and heard a dull metallic thud that was abruptly followed by a frantic burst in the pace of the engines. Rushing out on deck he found that the thick fog made it impossible to see anything at all. Twenty minutes later the fog showed signs of lifting and Second Officer Cummings, along with the rest of the ship's company, found themselves to be a centre of attraction.

'Imagine my horror when the first thing I saw was Hood Point Lighthouse and people standing on the shore looking at us. The fact that these people could be seen so clearly added to our dismay.'
The Cape Times, 25th December 1937

Even as two harbour tugs endeavoured to tow the *Stuart Star* clear, the ocean swell and the incoming tide combined to push against the starboard side of the ship, pinning her against the rocks. Practically the whole bottom of the hull from the engine-room to the bow had been ripped away. In the three forward holds there was more than 20 feet of water, and more was pouring into the engine-room and stokehold. The bilge, general service and transfer pumps were working at full power but could not cope with such a tremendous inrush of water. The tugs strained hard but, as tow rope after tow rope snapped like cotton threads, it was becoming a pointless exercise. Hundreds of people were now crowding the eastern slopes of the golf course, which was adjacent to the Indian Ocean. The *Stuart Star* was so close that she lay within easy driving range and, as the gallery of spectators swelled, the fog cleared completely, conveniently giving them a perfect day to watch the struggle to save the stricken ship. The main complaint in the bar of the clubhouse was the spectators were not members!

By 2 o'clock in the afternoon it was apparent that the pumps could no longer keep pace and 2 feet of rising oily water covered the engine-room floor. Keeping the boilers fired in those conditions was impossible and the order was given to abandon ship an hour later. The sea had calmed and the ninety-three crew and fifteen passengers were taken into Buffalo Harbour by lifeboat. This was accomplished in good time because as evening fell, the seas began to build up and crash against the ship, causing the steel hull to grind agonisingly against the rocks.

Finding emergency accommodation for the crew was not easy as most of the hotels in East London were booked for the Christmas season but, once settled in, most of them made their way to the scene of the wreck and sadly watched the death throes of their ship. A few days afterwards they were sent to Cape Town and assigned berths as Distressed British Seamen on board the liner *Dunbar Castle* which sailed for England on Christmas Day. Captain Sinclair, Chief Officer Rhodes and those on the bridge including the watch-keeping engineers, were required to stay behind and attend a Court of Marine Inquiry.

Captain Sinclair had two main points to make. Firstly, East London was the only port he was aware of that did not possess a fog warning apparatus. Hood Point was a very good lighthouse but its beam could not penetrate dense fog. (This was a valid point and a foghorn was later installed). Secondly, the pilot taking the *Balmoral Castle* into Buffalo Harbour was using the South African technique of having a tug continuously blow her whistle to act as a guide. This was a new procedure to Captain Sinclair and it had confused him. These points did not find much sympathy with the Chief Magistrate, Lieutenant-Commander RN and the Commodore of the Union Castle Line who made up the Board of Inquiry. Their verdict was that Captain Sinclair had failed '... to take the necessary precautions which ordinary careful navigation necessitates.' They had no choice but to order the suspension of Captain Sinclair's master's certificate.

Thus it was that the East London Golf Club, situated amongst some of the most picturesque hills and valleys of the South African seaboard, gained a unique landmark.

> 'For years afterwards, the bows of the *Stuart Star* were an East London landmark and thousands of South Africans had, over the years, come to East London to see the wreck.'
>
> *The Daily Despatch,* 12th August 1975.

Although the ship quickly broke up into three sections, the forepart remained next to the golf links and, on the bow, the name *Stuart Star* remained legible for decades. The wreck was also a prominent feature when seen from seaward and served as a reminder to every ship's master that harbour approaches can be dangerous places.

Chapter 16

A Master's Salvage

The crew of the S.S. *Nestor* liked to boast that the ship's 80-foot blue funnel, with its black top, was the tallest of any ship afloat. The cargo liner maintained a regular timetable plying the long ocean route from the United Kingdom to Australia. She was designed in the days when streamlining was unknown and reliability was taken for granted, and it was not until 1950 that the twin screw, veteran coal burner was scrapped after thirty-seven years of continuous service. The *Nestor* had sumptuous accommodation for two hundred and fifty first-class passengers and had a commodious dining saloon enabling all the passengers to dine together. The vessel was fitted throughout with oak, and with a spacious promenade boatdeck she was a favourite with passengers. Tickets were expensive, but Blue Funnel ships were very popular and her cabins were invariably fully booked. Cargo was an important part of the Blue Funnel Line's operations and the *Nestor* had the capacity to carry 15,000 tons in her five cargo holds. She held a special place in many British and Australian hearts, and newspapers of the day described her as 'the large Blue Funnel Line steamer *Nestor*' – she was indeed an imposing sight.

In June 1936, under the command of Captain J.J. Power, the *Nestor* was once again homeward-bound from Australia. One of her last ports of call was Adelaide and on 21st June the ship ran into a severe winter gale about 200 miles south of her destination. The atrocious weather did not ease and by mid-afternoon Captain Power was forced to stop the liner and heave to. With the rough sea making life uncomfortable, many of the passengers decided to forego the evening meal and retreated to their cabins. The *Nestor* remained hove to and at 6.04 pm she received a very loud and clear SOS from the S.S. *Mungana*, an Australian freighter that was being swept onto rocks less than 10 miles distant.

As the master of a British ship, Captain Power had a duty to proceed with all speed to the assistance of a vessel in distress upon receiving a call for help. What he was able to do when he arrived there would be up to him. He was responsible not only for the safety of his vessel, but also for the lives of the two hundred and fifty-five passengers and crew. The *Mungana* had a crew of forty-eight and it was clear that she was completely disabled. Her anchor chains had snapped and she was in danger of being swept onto a rocky shore. Captain Power ordered all hands on deck and every lifeboat was made ready for launching. It is against any mariner's instinct to steer towards a lee shore on a dark, stormy night, but the die was cast, and turning the ship into the teeth of the gale, he went to their assistance. Extra men were stationed as lookouts and the ship's powerful searchlights were switched on. In addition, the second officer and bosun were in charge of a volunteer boat's crew and they were ready to risk their lives in a rescue attempt. A buzz of excited conversation swept through the passengers and some of them braved the elements to venture out on deck to see what was happening.

The S.S. *Mungana* was an ageing freighter owned by the Australian Union Steam Navigation Co. (AUSN), less than half the size of the *Nestor*. She only traded between Australian ports and had left Adelaide the day before bound for Queensland with 2,400 tons of general cargo. On leaving harbour she had run into the heavy weather that was lashing the south Australian coast and having constantly to thrash her way through high seas, her engine thrust bearing gave way which disabled her. South-westerly gales took hold of the ship and began to pummel her towards the shore. Both anchors were let go but the chains parted under the strain and the *Mungana* quickly headed towards the Margaret Brock reef just a few miles away. A similar mishap had happened to the *Lindenbank* on almost the same stretch of coast the previous November. It took only half-an-hour before the senior officers high up in the wheelhouse of the *Nestor* were able to fix the position of the *Mungana*. Through the rain squalls and increasing darkness, the wildly swaying masthead lights of the freighter were visible only fleetingly. Close by, to the south, came the rhythmic flash of the Cape Jaffa Lighthouse, a metal structure that stood at the northern end of the Margaret Brock reef. From his position out on the bridge wing 90 feet above the sea, Captain Power felt the full strength of the 60 mph gusts and knew that whatever he decided to do would involve some risk. To try and pick up the crew from the *Mungana* in the appalling conditions was to attempt the impossible. In order to save the crew he would have to save the ship, and to do that a line would have to be placed on board to tow her clear.

In the howling winds and high seas firing a line by rocket gun was going to be a hit and miss affair, but Captain Power decided to try. Signalling to Captain P.H. Day, long-time master of the *Mungana,* he took the *Nestor* in towards the shoreline and as close as he dared to the freighter which was rolling unpredictably. Using his judgement, the *Nestor'*s third officer fired a number of rockets but each one was overcome by the gale force winds and blown away into the night.

On board the *Mungana,* Second Officer Pratt assumed a similar responsibility and fired a number of rockets upwards towards the towering decks of the Blue Funnel liner, but without success. The ships passed and Captain Power called a halt to the rocket firing – there was only a limited supply and another method of securing a line would have to be tried. His chief officer suggested they float a line downwind on a lighted lifebuoy and he left the bridge to supervise this, but again, due to the severe weather conditions, its direction could not be controlled and the buoy was quickly swamped. The next idea was to make a small raft with a sail and light and, with a line attached to it, it would hopefully be blown

The master of the Nestor *accepted grave risks, not only to his ship, but to his crew and passengers, when he successfully salvaged a freighter being blown onto a rocky shore.* Photograph courtesy of the Arbon-Le Maistre collection, State Library of South Australia.

towards the *Mungana*. The contraption was thrown overboard, where it spun around and promptly disintegrated.

Impatient with these failures, Captain Power was fighting to keep the *Nestor* in position. It was exhausting work, with constant helm and engine commands, but he ceaselessly fought against the elements that buffeted his ship. By using the ship's twin screws independently of each other he had a manoeuvrability that a single-screw steamer lacked, but nevertheless it was a demanding task. A Morse signal flashed from the lighthouse to warn Captain Power that his ship was getting too close to the reefs and, against his better judgement, he decided to chance sending a lifeboat across the chasm of the raging seas to the *Mungana*. Blue Funnel Line lifeboats were sturdier than most, being built especially for the company at Hong Kong by skilled boatbuilders. If one could be launched and handled well, then with luck a line could be taken to the freighter. The *Nestor* made a lee as the boat's crew took their places at the oars, and at a word from the second officer the boat was expertly lowered into the sea. The small white lifeboat could faintly be seen twisting and corkscrewing up and over each successive wave, but, in spite of some hard pulling on the oars, it looked as if the boat would be overwhelmed at any second. The second officer thought so too and, waiting for the right moment, he turned around and struggled back to the shelter of the *Nestor*. As the boat's crew scrambled up the rope ladders which were flung over the ship's side, Bosun Owen Murphy lost his grip and was nearly swept away. Relieved that no lives had been lost in this futile venture, Captain Power decided that he must take *Nestor* in closer and use the remaining rockets to shoot a line on board the helpless *Mungana*. It was a grave risk, but unless he took it Captain Day and his crew were surely going to lose their lives.

A flurry of wireless messages outlined Captain Power's bold intentions and Captain Day confirmed that his ship would fire every rocket she had in a last ditch attempt to get a line secured. The beginnings of a bleak dawn were welcomed as it would make distances easier to judge and the *Nestor* cautiously began to approach the storm-tossed freighter. The sailors on both ships stood tense and alert to grab any rocket line that came close to them. Captain Power knew that he had to succeed – there would not be another chance. The Blue Funnel liner dwarfed the *Mungana* and came so close, as one awed passenger later put it

'We could have thrown a threepenny piece onto the decks of the disabled steamer.'

The Advertiser, 24th June 1936.

In fact they passed so close that the *Mungana* rolled against the *Nestor* causing some superficial damage. A volley of rocket fire was exchanged and the captain, concentrating on handling his ship, could only hope fervently that a rocket had been landed successfully. Suddenly the sound of hoarse cheering reached his ears and he knew that his persistence had been rewarded.

Of all the rockets fired, only the very last one from the *Mungana* had proved its worth. Second Mate Pratt had given up all hope when he took the only remaining rocket from its red wooden box and loaded it into the hand-held gun. The *Nestor* was passing and would not be coming back, so he took aim and fired. This rocket, unlike the others, was blessed with good luck and fizzed up and landed on the after deck of the *Nestor*. Eager hands seized it and hauled in the light line that was attached to it. Gradually the thin lifeline was replaced by a thicker one until eventually the eye of the thick wire hawser was hauled across from the freighter to the stern of the larger ship. With the reef looming ever closer, it was time to secure the hawser and start the tow. It was broad daylight as the *Nestor* tentatively towed the *Mungana* to seaward, before turning north-west and slowly steaming towards Port Adelaide 170 miles away. Approaching harbour she handed over the freighter to a tug and on entering was greeted by a colourful display of signal flags that spelt out: 'Congratulations, Nestor', and accompanying blasts of numerous ships' sirens.

The possibility of a claim for salvage services had not been considered by Captain Power when he went to the assistance of the *Mungana* – saving the lives of fellow seafarers had been his only concern. Nevertheless, five months later in London, a large salvage award of £11,750 was made (£8,000 to the Blue Funnel Line as owners of the *Nestor*, £1,000 to Captain Power and £2,750 to the officers and crew) and the presiding judge, who had determined the amount of the awards, was moved to comment:

'It was a very plucky service, rendered in very dangerous conditions, and was essentially a master's salvage.'

Chapter 17

A Strange Stowaway

In 1920 Alexander Smith passed the examination for his master's certificate in Aberdeen. He soon found employment as a chief officer and for three-and-a-half years showed great potential while serving on a variety of tramp steamers, but was unable to settle down with any particular company. In January 1925 his luck changed and his career took a turn for the better.

Named after Fenchurch Avenue in the heart of the City of London, the Avenue Shipping Company appointed Alexander Smith chief officer of their first and brand new motor ship, the *Enton*. He joined the vessel in February 1925 for her maiden voyage to Australia, and settled in so well that he spent the following years on long tramping voyages to Australia and the west coast of America. Being a thoroughly modern ship, the *Enton* was always in profitable employment and the company decided to purchase a second ship in 1928. This was a newly-built motor-ship named *Winton* (see chapter 26). The expansion of the Avenue Shipping Co. benefited Alexander Smith because Christopher Mordaunt, master of the *Enton,* transferred to the *Winton* and Chief Officer Smith, who had proved so trustworthy and reliable, was given command of the *Enton.*

Captain Smith's first voyage as master was in October 1928 taking the *Enton* on another long and familiar haul to Australia and North America. Two years passed with similar voyages and, with such an excellent ship and generous owners, Alexander Smith was enjoying life and looked forward to being in command of the *Enton* for a long time to come.

October 1930 found the *Enton* at Rotterdam and, signing on as a member of the crew, according to the 'Agreement and Account of Crew', was Captain Smith's wife, Christina. She was thirty-eight, the same age as her husband, and this was her first trip to sea. According to the document this was for '... a voyage of not exceeding two years duration to any ports or places within the limits of 75 degrees north and 60 degrees south latitude, commencing at Rotterdam proceeding thence to New York and New Zealand and/or any other ports within the above limits, trading in any rotation, and to end at such port in the United Kingdom or Continent or Europe as may be required by the master'.

To conform with the Board of Trade Regulations she had to sign on as a stewardess and was looking forward to an around-the-world voyage with her husband. The ship was to load case oil (petrol in 5-gallon cans packed in wooden crates) at New York bound for New Zealand and New Caledonia and then, having completed the discharge, load heavy chrome ore at Pagoumene (New Caledonia) finishing off with copra from the Pacific Islands for the Continent.

The voyage proceeded as planned, with a two-week stay in New York, a short call at Newport News and then a non-stop, 36-day passage to New Zealand. Consignments of case oil were delivered to Auckland, Wellington and Lyttleton, and then, with the last 1,000 tons of cargo in her holds, the ship sailed for Noumea. A stowaway who had slipped on board at Lyttleton was soon discovered and Captain Smith had little option but to sign him on. He was an Australian from New South Wales named Arthur Rowe. His strange manner and insistence that he would be going to Australia earned him the nickname Jonah.

After crossing the Tropic of Capricorn, Captain Smith pulled out the Admiralty chart *Nouvelle Calédonie* in preparation for the approach to Noumea. Port Noumea is fronted by an extensive barrier of reefs around which strong tidal currents swirl and rip with unpredictable force. The main approach through the great reef is Bulari Passage, which is marked by a lighthouse off the southern end of the reefs on Amedee Island, about 100 miles south-east of Noumea. It was Captain Smith's intention to steer the recommended course parallel to the reefs until he picked up the flash of the Amedee Lighthouse in the early hours of 28th January. The ship would then wait for the pilot to take charge for the last 12 miles through the reef-encumbered waters and into harbour.

By midnight the sky was an inky black with clouds completely covering the stars, making celestial observation impossible. It was a time of great concern for Captain Smith. With no way to fix his position accurately he was uneasy about the unlit and dangerous reefs that stretched away to starboard. When Second Mate Mandle came on watch at midnight he found Captain Smith frequently consulting Walker's patent log and ensuring that the helmsman maintained course.

The 'graveyard' watch of 12–4 am was nearing its end and with the Amedee

Lighthouse still at least 30 miles ahead, Captain Smith was unsure of his position. He had just made up his mind to give the reefs more sea room when, with an ear-splitting screech, the bow of the *Enton* lifted and the ship slithered onto a reef. The engines were stopped immediately and the crew tumbled out on deck and gathered around the ship's port and starboard lifeboats. The soft rhythmic sound of breakers could be heard but, apart from that, the warm darkness revealed nothing.

The *Enton* had driven onto a flat reef and sat upright, lying quietly and taking very little water. Daybreak revealed a dark circle of rocky reefs with smooth seas breaking lazily over them. Although the ship was stuck fast, she was not in any danger and perhaps, if her remaining 1,000 tons of case oil could be dumped, she might float off at high tide. With this in mind, Captain Smith radioed his position as being aground on Ambuie Reef, 53 miles south of

High and dry on a reef near Noumea, the wreck of the Enton *was a prominent feature for many years.* Photograph courtesy of the State Library of South Australia.

Noumea. He requested assistance and asked that lighters and a local steamer be sent from Port Numea so that the case oil, which was a much-needed commodity, could be saved. The rest of the day was spent waiting for help to arrive, but during the night the weather changed dramatically and angry seas crashed against the high and exposed hull of the freighter, the stronger swells surging beneath the ship and lifting her. At first it was hoped that the waves might lift the Enton clear and Captain Smith resisted the urge to drop anchor to hold her fast. Instead, he used the engine to advantage in trying to free the ship but, by the morning of the 28th the ship was in a worse predicament, especially as she was now taking water in the forward holds. A heavy swell was making the vessel bump alarmingly and Captain Smith realized that only a powerful salvage tug would have any real chance of towing his ship free. Whilst the Avenue Shipping Company and Lloyds underwriters in London endeavoured to secure the services of a tug from Brisbane, all hopes were pinned on help arriving from Noumea.

Thursday, 29th January was to prove a day that none of the crew of the *Enton* would ever forget. Expecting the arrival of a small steamer towing a lighter from Noumea, a party of seamen were busy lowering a lifeboat in readiness to assist in the task of bringing the lighter alongside. A heavy lifeboat had been lowered and was being tethered to the ship by an extra long rope, the end of which lay coiled on deck. Suddenly, the lifeboat was caught by a massive swell and shot off like a rocket, the rope searing through a sailor's hands and entwining itself around one of his legs. Shrieking in agony, he could do nothing as his foot was severed, and then his leg was ripped off above the knee. It was a horrific accident. Men rushed to his aid and a crude tourniquet was twisted around the torn limb to stem the gushing blood. He was carried into the saloon where he was given a quantity of brandy and Mrs Smith did her best to comfort him and prevent him from tearing off the tourniquet.

Later in the afternoon, the island steamer *Saint Vincent de Paul* arrived towing a lighter. The *Enton* kept moving as the ocean swells lifted her, but perversely the same swells made transferring the cargo out of the question. Also the island steamer was so under-powered that any hopes of using her to tow the *Enton* evaporated. With evening drawing on, the mortally-injured seaman mercifully lapsed into a coma and died. Since the prospects of saving the ship were slim, Captain Smith decided to send his wife and the crew ashore, along with the body of the seaman. Chief Officer Edwin Morris stayed behind with his skipper to await the anticipated arrival of the Australian salvage team. Once in Noumea the shipwrecked mariners quickly found berths on *Laperouse*, a ship that traded regularly between Sydney and New Caledonia and along with them went Arthur Rowe.

'Wreck of the *Enton*
Crew reaches Sydney
A gripping story of the wreck of the motor ship *Enton*, which struck
the Amadu Reef on 28 January, was told by the 30 members of the
crew who arrived by the *Laperouse* yesterday. The men, who
appeared none the worse for their experience, were in charge of the
Second Officer, Mr. W.B. Mandle. Gloomily they attributed their
bad luck and the wreck to the 'Jonah' influence of a stowaway who
embarked at Lyttleton, New Zealand, the ship's last port of call'.

Sydney Morning Herald, 12th February 1931

Remaining on board the *Enton*, Captain Smith and Chief Officer Morris spent
a lonely vigil like two lighthouse keepers. The days of waiting ended on 3rd
March when two Australian salvage experts, acting on instructions from Lloyds
and the Salvage Association in London, came on board to assess the situation.
They found the remarkable phenomenon of an ocean freighter lying practically
undamaged on top of a flat reef an extraordinary sight. Their professional
instincts told them that if salvage operations had commenced sooner the vessel
would certainly have been refloated. Since the cargo was worth in excess of
£10,000 they judged that a belated salvage attempt would be financially justified.
They proposed to proceed on a 'no cure, no pay' basis and planned to hire a
steamer from Noumea together with lighters and fifty labourers to retrieve the
1,000 tons of case oil. Next, a number of three-ton anchors would be laid out
from the bow and on the highest tide the ship would use her windlass to heave
herself across the reef and into deep water. Her engine-room was undamaged
and if the huge diesel engine could be persuaded to start they would have all the
power they needed to work the ship free. Once the *Enton* was officially in the
hands of the salvors, Captain Smith and Chief Officer Morris were released
from their duties. For Captain Smith it was a particularly poignant farewell to
the ship in which he had spent six happy years.

Later, in the London office of the Avenue Shipping Company, Alexander Smith
found the management sympathetic. The waters around the reefs of New Caledonia
had justly acquired a very bad reputation, and it was accepted that the ship had
been swept off course by a violent side current. On learning that all attempts to
salvage the *Enton* had failed, he wondered if he would ever command a ship again.

However, four years later he was back at sea until March 1943 when he was
killed by enemy aircraft fire whilst in command of M.V. *Empire Charmian*. He
was buried in Italy and commended for war services.

Chapter 18

Narrative of Operations

In the Admiralty files held in the Public Record Office, London, is the log book and narrative of operations belonging to HMS *Frobisher* from January 1935. These documents give an exciting account of a 900-mile tow from mid-Atlantic to the island of Bermuda.

Gow, Harrison & Co. of Gordon Street, Glasgow were well-known as tanker tramp ship owners. At the end of 1934 the latest addition to their fleet was the *Valverda*, built on the Clyde and fitted with two massive diesel engines which gave the tanker a speed of 13 knots. There was keen competition for a berth on the new ship, for her accommodation was first-class and the company was known to operate its ships across the Atlantic rather than to the red-hot furnace of the Persian Gulf.

Although Captain Thomas, master of the *Valverda*, was no stranger to the busy oil-loading berths of Curacao, he seldom had any free time to spend ashore. Tanker crews had come to accept that quick turnrounds on the outskirts of the world's oil ports gave little opportunity for shore leave. A few warm days and nights impregnated with the overpowering smell of crude oil and a brief impression of the canals and Dutch-style houses of Willemstad, was as much as most tankermen knew of Curacao.

Being a new ship, the *Valverda* stood out from the assortment of tankers waiting their turn to load. Her gleaming paintwork and bright red funnel made her one of the best-looking tankers flying the Red Ensign. On 14th January 1935, loaded with 13,246 tons of crude oil and petroleum spirit, the ship left the Netherlands Antilles. She crossed the Caribbean and headed out into the Atlantic bound for Hamburg. Her oil cargo was worth £20,000 – about one third of the value of the ship.

A week later in mid-Atlantic a fierce outbreak of fire, probably caused by a leaking oil-feed pipe, erupted in the engine-room and completely disabled the main engine and steering gear. The tanker was not only at the mercy of the brooding Atlantic, but flames were also threatening to reach the oil and turn the tanker into a floating fireball. The third and fifth engineers had both been badly burnt whilst courageously shutting off the fuel supply to the diesel engines, and their bravery gave the rest of the crew a fighting chance to tackle the fire. The heat was so fierce that it caused the forward bulkhead of the engine-room to buckle badly and actually melted the cylinder tops of the two main engines. Unnoticed by anyone in the darkness, the ship's wooden lifeboats had been destroyed by the fire and Captain Thomas knew then it was time to think about sending out an SOS. 460 miles away the frantic signal was picked by HMS *Frobisher*, a cruiser serving as a cadets' training ship, and outward bound from Chatham to Port of Spain, Trinidad. The drama was quickly reported by newspapers across the world.

'Ships racing to blazing tanker'.
Herald Special Representative, London.

'Six merchantmen and a British training cruiser, the *Frobisher*, are racing full speed to the rescue of the British oil tanker, *Valverda*, which is 1,000 miles off the coast of Florida'.
The Melbourne Herald, *22nd January 1935.*

At 4.20 am on a cold and overcast morning, *Frobisher* was easily riding the Atlantic swells steering 232° and making 12 knots. Captain Piers Kekewich, RN, commanding the ship, studied the SOS that had just been received from the *Valverda*. Other shipping in the area was responding and it was initially unclear if the cruiser was the best-placed vessel to render assistance. After careful evaluation and the fact that *Frobisher* had the potential to steam at 30 knots, Captain Kekewich ordered full speed ahead and altered course to 267° to go to *Valverda's* aid. One hundred miles astern of the cruiser, and also en route for Port of Spain, was the net layer, HMS *Guardian*. She was ordered to alter course and follow her larger consort.

By 7.30 am on Monday, 21st January *Frobisher* was plunging at high speed through heavy seas and although the crashing waves caused some minor damage, the warship handled magnificently. All through the day and into the night the cruiser hammered her way south-westwards, speed being slightly reduced to reach the *Valverda* in daylight. Wireless communications suggested that the fire on the tanker was under control (mainly due to huge waves sweeping across her decks), and Captain Thomas proposed that his ship be taken in tow. Captain Kekewich was authorized by the Admiralty to undertake the tow because the tanker was in grave danger of becoming a derelict or even a total loss.

At 7am the following day, *Frobisher* sighted the disabled tanker and steamed in close under her lee to examine her. The deeply-laden *Valverda* was lying in the trough of the sea with waves breaking across her two tank decks. Her stern was burnt and blackened with wisps of smoke occasionally billowing up out of the engine-room skylight, but she appeared to be in no danger of sinking. Arrangements for taking the tanker in tow were already in place on the pointed after-end of the cruiser's quarter-deck. The towing cable was ready to be passed out through the starboard fair-lead to be shackled to one of *Valverda*'s anchor chains. As a precaution, a seaboat's crew was standing by to take off the tanker's 36-man crew if she started to sink.

Working feverishly on the wildly dipping and rolling fo'c's'le head of the tanker, her crew at last succeeded in making the port anchor fast and unshackled the cable ready to attach the towing wire from *Frobisher*. Captain Kekewich slowly circled the wallowing tanker until all was ready. In London, the Admiralty had agreed to a request made by Gow, Harrison Co. to tow their tanker 900 miles to Bermuda. *Frobisher* passed close by the bow of the tanker and a line was fired across by rocket gun. This was eagerly seized by those on the fo'c's'le head and, as there was no steam on the windlass, the heavy 6½-inch towing wire had to be hauled hand over hand across the yawning gap between the two ships. It was backbreaking work, but by noon the tow was fast. With her engines at slow ahead, *Frobisher* slowly took up the strain. The *Valverda* was heavy and sluggish and, with no steering to ease the burden, the strain on her windlass was massive. After exactly twelve minutes the brake on the windlass gave way, allowing the anchor cable to fly out of the locker and snap off in the hawsepipe. The complete towing wire with eight shackles of anchor chain hanging on the end of it swung like a pendulum from the cruiser's stern. Instantly aware that if this wire became entangled around any of the warship's four propeller shafts it would cripple his ship, Captain Kekewich ordered the whole lot to be released.

In the early afternoon HMS *Guardian* arrived and successfully attached a towing wire to the *Valverda*. After a few hours of trying to haul the tanker around to the north-west, this wire snapped and the two warships spent an uncomfortable night keeping out of each other's way. During the night the *Valverda's* third engineer died and the rest of the crew weighed up their own

The disabled Valverda *wallows in the Atlantic swell as* H.M.S. Frobisher *stands by to take her in tow.* Photograph courtesy of the State Library of South Australia.

chances of survival. It was clear that unless the *Valverda* could be made to steer, no towing wire would be strong enough to hold her. For the next two days bad weather prevented any further attempts at towing. This delay was put to good use by fabricating fittings in the *Guardian*'s workshop that would, in theory, enable the rudder of the *Valverda* to be turned by hand.

A marked improvement in the weather ended the hours of waiting and on Friday 25th January at 8.45 am, a cutter was lowered from *Frobisher* with the express purpose of reporting on the state of the *Valverda*'s electric-hydraulic steering system. It was quickly established that the main engine was beyond repair but, with Royal Naval expertise and equipment, the steering could be made to turn. The cutter shuttled backwards and forwards, taking the badly-burnt fifth engineer to the sick bay and ferrying the specially-engineered fittings from *Guardian*. A party of seven officers and specialist ratings were placed on the tanker with orders to get the steering gear working. It was due mainly to their efforts that salvage of the *Valverda* was possible, because even minimal use of the rudder was an improvement on none at all.

At this point the *Guardian* was ordered to proceed to St. Lucia but there was a delay whilst a thick towing wire was transferred to *Frobisher* to replace the one that had been lost. With *Guardian* gone, Captain Kekewich was faced with an extremely challenging task. To propose to tow a fully-laden tanker 900 miles across the Atlantic in winter was challenge enough, but to use a cruiser that had been designed for speed and attack added an extra dimension. The repairs to the steering gear meant that the tanker now had limited use of her rudder to counteract the swinging of the ship's head and gradually the two vessels moved ahead in unison. Over the next six days, strong following winds and a day of calm enabled the warship to tow the tanker at an average speed of 5 knots, and on the afternoon of Thursday, 31st January Gibbs Lighthouse on the startlingly-green island of Bermuda was sighted. The entrance into the harbour anchorage had not been named the Narrows without good reason, and it would be unthinkable for *Frobisher* to lose her prize now.

After spending an uneasy night drifting offshore, the next day was full of activity rearranging the towing arrangements to run the gauntlet of the Narrows. The towing wire was shortened and an Admiralty dockyard tug, *Sandboy,* was secured alongside the tanker to steady her up. Another smaller Admiralty tug, *Creole,* assisted in rigging up a second tow line, and when Captain Kekewich was satisfied that all was ready, he signalled that he was about to enter harbour. There was a fairly strong wind and moderate swell as *Frobisher* made a wide circle in order to get a straight run at the entrance. At the appropriate time Captain Kekewich ordered an increase in speed and steered directly for the Narrows, taking exactly 28 minutes to pull the *Valverda* into the quiet waters of Murray's Anchorage. It had been a splendid achievement and the Royal Navy had gone well beyond 'rendering assistance'. They had made an all-out effort to salvage a valuable ship and her cargo. To commemorate this remarkable operation, the owners of the *Valverda* gratefully presented a large silver bowl to HMS *Frobisher.* The inscription reads:

'Presented to the officers and men of HMS Frobisher by Gow, Harrison & Co and managers of the TSMV *Valverda*, Glasgow, in recognition of the gallant services they rendered in January 1935.'

Chapter 19

Running out of Coal

On a cold Christmas Day, Newcastle-upon-Tyne in 1932, the festivities of three elderly brothers – F.W., B.E. and L.A. Common – were interrupted. They were well-known shipowners who traded as the Common Brothers and one of their ships was in trouble.

'S.S. *Newbrough* ashore Morant Cay, water all holds, engine-room. Abandoned by crew'.

The brothers were puzzled. It was the first peace-time loss the company had suffered in twenty-seven years of trading and Captain Norman Smith, master of the *Newbrough*, was one of their most experienced and favourite officers. They spent the rest of the day waiting impatiently for further details.

Operating a tramp shipping company during a trade depression required owners to make difficult decisions and to insist on strict economies. To secure a homeward cargo of grain, it had necessitated sending the *Newbrough* in ballast from Montreal to Vancouver. When she arrived on 24th November another company ship, the *Rajahstan,* was already under the elevators taking on wheat in bulk and the *Newbrough* tied up behind her. Loading was quick and, after a long 35-day passage from Montreal, the crew was anxious for shore leave. They were getting to know Vancouver well, for it was the third time that the ship had called there that year. A cargo of 8,000 tons of Manitoba wheat was taken on board and after only three days in port the tramp steamer was underway again bound for Hull. In ballast, the ship had risen to the waves, but now, making the 4,000-mile Pacific Ocean passage towards Panama, she was sluggish and heavy, with green seas constantly sweeping over her foredeck.

When it was doubtful that there was sufficient coal to reach her designated port, the S.S. Newbrough *was forced to alter course to fill up her bunkers, and as a consequence the ship was wrecked.* Photograph courtesy of the World Ship Photo Library.

Captain Norman Smith, aged forty-one and master of the *Newbrough* for over two years, did not usually concern himself with the workings of the engine-room (in the Merchant Navy engine-rooms were strictly the province of chief engineers). Yet with volumes of black smoke pouring from the funnel and with the ship's progress being constantly hampered by wind and sea, he became troubled about excessive fuel consumption. However, Chief Engineer Charles Pickard assured him that all was well. He had joined the ship earlier in the year and he and Captain Smith had spent the previous voyage to Vancouver accompanied by their wives and the captain's seven-year-old daughter, Norma. The two men had formed a friendship although their professional duties left little time for socializing.

The company's standing orders were for the *Newbrough* to pass through the Panama Canal and take on bunkers at the island of St. Thomas in the Virgin

Islands. The economies of fuelling the ship were controlled by the Common brothers and left no margin for error or waste. Buying coal at a non-approved port was strictly frowned upon by all tramp ship owners and, knowing this, Captain Smith relied upon his chief engineer to have enough coal in reserve to reach the designated bunker port. The *Newbrough* left the canal and dropped the pilot at Colon where Chief Engineer Pickard checked the bunkers to satisfy himself that there was enough coal to reach St. Thomas. Sometimes heavy weather would burn coal with no distance made, or a hidden patch of slack would not burn, upsetting calculations. Invariably coal would be hoarded for such emergencies for if a ship did run out the consequences could be disastrous.

Second Mate Joseph Swinsco of Leamington-on-Tyne had joined the *Newbrough* in March after serving as second mate on another of the company's ships. Thomas Mitchell, aged twenty, joined the ship at the same time for his first trip as a Third Mate. On British ships the second mate was traditionally the navigating officer and responsible for fixing the ship's daily position. Noon sights were never to be missed (weather permitting) and the ship's progress was recorded from noon to noon.

James Lindsay, aged seventeen, was one of four deck apprentices carried by the *Newbrough* and he had been placed in the 12–4 watch to assist and learn the art of navigation from Second Mate Swinsco. It was the usual practice for an apprentice to keep a lookout whilst the officer of the watch worked out his sights or wrote up the log book in the chartroom. It was a routine that was repeated every day and night.

On 19th December Limon Bay slipped astern and the *Newbrough* steamed unhurriedly into the Caribbean. Captain Smith received a wireless message that made him a trifle uneasy. The *Rajahstan,* also calling at St. Thomas, was only a day ahead and reported that she was experiencing heavy weather. It was a friendly warning from one ship's master to another, but in this case Captain Smith was aware of the need to conserve fuel. As expected, the seas began to rise and speed was reduced as the tramp struggled to make headway. This spell of rough weather ate into the coal reserves but the *Newbrough* was soon pushing through a brilliant blue and flat calm sea. The officers' saloon and crew's mess had been festooned with Christmas decorations and all hands were looking forward to a special Christmas dinner. As an extra bonus, the ship's wireless officer had promised he would ensure that the whole crew could listen to King George V make the first-ever Christmas Day broadcast to the British Empire.

In the engine-room it was the trimmers, whose job it was to fetch the coal from the bunkers to the stokehold, who sounded the alarm. The bunkers were getting dangerously low and mixed in with the last of the coal was tons of dust and muck which had lain concealed under layers of good coal for many voyages. Chief Engineer Pickard took his flashlight and descended into the dark recesses of the main cross bunker. He checked the port and starboard wing bunkers and came to the unwelcome conclusion that there was less than 80 tons of decent coal left.

Captain Smith listened with some annoyance as Charles Pickard explained that unfortunately much of the coal in the bunkers was rubbish and would not burn. The ship's current latitude and longitude were quickly plotted on the chart with some startling results. They were over 600 miles from Colon, 530 miles from St. Thomas and 415 miles from Kingston. There was barely enough coal in the bunkers to take them to Kingston, a bunkering port sometimes used by the Common Brothers Line.

Knowing that a ship on charter was not permitted to deviate from her course except under exceptional circumstances, he assumed that running out of coal was sufficient reason. He therefore altered course for Kingston where he could easily take on extra coal. Trusting to the weather, he anticipated that the ship would arrive around midday on 24th December, the crew at least being delighted at the prospect of spending Christmas at Kingston.

Just past noon on 22nd December, the *Newbrough* made a 90° diversion from her course and steered toward the eastern tip of Jamaica. Ships rarely approached Kingston from the east as many dangerous low-lying reefs and rocks were scattered far out from the coast. The unlit Albatross Bank, Morant Cays, Pedro Bank and Alice Shoal were to be given a wide berth at all times, especially at night. Around these shoals and reefs variable and strong currents could push or pull a ship far off her intended course. Noon sights taken by the ship's officers placed the steamer 200 miles nearer to Jamaica and, with 30 tons of coal left, another twenty-four hours should see the vessel safely docked amongst the hotchpotch of wharves and jetties that made up Kingston Harbour. Her course was adjusted to pass 15 miles south of the notorious Morant Cays that lie in the sea 32 miles off the Jamaican coast. On his own initiative, Second Mate Swinsco took an evening star sight at 5.55 pm which put the Cays 80 miles ahead. Captain Smith checked the ship's position on the chart and stayed on the bridge with the relatively inexperienced Third Mate Mitchell until the change of watch at midnight. After he had given clear instructions to Second Mate Swinsco to alter course by 4° at 2 am in order to keep clear of the Morant Cays, he turned in for a few hours sleep with orders to be called immediately in the event of anything happening.

Mindful of his forthcoming examination for his master's ticket, Joseph Swinsco decided to concentrate on fixing the ship's position as accurately as possible. He took a number of star sights and went into the chartroom to work them out. Engrossed in calculations, it slipped his mind to alter course by 4° at 2 am. Forty minutes passed before he remembered and, to compensate, he altered course by 8°. After seeing that all was well he went back into the chartroom.

The apprentice's duty was to keep lookout for the second officer. He regularly scanned the dim horizon and, by watching the ship's foremast in relation to the position of the stars, he could check how well the helmsman was steering. It was 3.30 am and Second Mate Swinsco had been in and out of the chartroom for most of the watch. Alone, James Lindsay stared through the wheelhouse windows – there seemed to be a long, horizontal white line ahead. Puzzled, he concentrated his gaze. It was not starlight, it was phosphorescence. It was the sea breaking over something! He turned and hurried into the chartroom.

Second Mate Swinsco looked up and curtly acknowledged the apprentice's report. He left the chart table and entered the wheelhouse, his eyes taking a short time to adjust. He stood for several minutes trying to make sense of what he saw, reluctant to take the responsibility of stopping the ship. Deciding to call the captain, he turned and hurried down the stairs to his cabin and, as he did so, there was a tremendous crash as the ship slammed into a reef. Captain Smith was out of his cabin and up to the wheelhouse in a moment. The telegraph was put to stop and it took only a moment for an anguished Captain Smith to comprehend what had happened.

Chief Officer Halliday and Third Mate Mitchell burst into the wheelhouse and Chief Engineer Pickard also appeared and announced that the engine-room was flooding. The breaking surf and strong swells began to make the trapped ship grind heavily on the reef and it was obvious that the ship could not withstand it for long. Captain Smith quickly regained his composure, ordered the lifeboats to be swung out and gave the ship's position to the wireless operator who began tapping out a series of calls for assistance.

It was Saturday 24th December and the time was just after 4 am. The SOS was answered straight away by the cableship *Norseman* of London which had just left Kingston bound for St. Lucia, and six hours later she arrived at the scene. Captain Sherwood, the master of the *Norseman,* cautiously anchored his ship 1½ miles off the south-east edge of the Morant Cay and sent in a lifeboat. The *Newbrough* was trapped in the middle of a tangle of reefs with seas breaking all round her. The tramp steamer was broadside on to the seas which at times were crashing over the decks and superstructure so that it was impossible to put a lifeboat alongside her. Likewise, she could not safely use her own hefty lifeboats. Communication by wireless established that the tramp ship was close enough to an exposed section of reef and sandbank to get a lifeline ashore. If that could be done it would give the crew a chance to escape from the ship and take refuge until the lifeboat could pick them up.

This seemed to be a workable plan and Chief Officer Halliday took charge of a small dinghy with a handful of volunteers and successfully rode the surf to land on the cay. He prepared to receive a line fired by rocket gun from the *Newbrough* but the wind was too strong and every rocket failed to find its target. Meanwhile, hovering off the seaward side of the cay the large lifeboat from the *Norseman* could see the men, but could not find a safe landing place. The rescue attempt was at a stalemate, but determined that something had to be done, Ernest Halliday tied a light line around his waist and swam courageously against the breakers towards the lifeboat. Although he was beaten back, his brave example encouraged Antonio Viana, bosun of the *Norseman,* to dive from the lifeboat with a line and allow himself to be swept by the breakers to the rocky shore. The line he carried was attached to a heavier one and this would act as a lifeline for the shipwrecked crew.

The next task was to land the remaining crew from the tramp ship onto the exposed cay. Observing an opening in the reefs between the cay and the ship, Ernest Halliday once again took the initiative and swam strongly out towards the *Newbrough.* After some hesitation they realized that the chief officer was signalling to them that they could use the lifeboat to come ashore. Guided by his hand signals, the ship's lifeboat was launched and, with Captain Smith at the tiller, the remainder of the crew were safely landed on the cay. Captain Smith was the first to shake the hand of his chief officer, telling him, "You're a brave man, Mister, and a strong swimmer too!" Chief Officer Halliday and Bosun Viana were subsequently both awarded the Board of Trade Sea Gallantry Medal.

Safely on board the *Norseman,* Captain Smith was able to send a brief cable to the Common brothers. At that moment he was unable to let them know the details of how their ship had ended up a total wreck on the Morant Cay as a result of running out of coal.

Chapter 20

His Guardian Angel

A t the end of December 1936, the tramp ship S.S. *Kingswood* was sweltering at anchor a few miles from Port Pirie, South Australia. It was wheat harvesting time and steamers and windjammers were gathering to take away the new season's crop. The *Kingswood* was chartered to load a cargo of 7,500 tons of ore concentrates and was held up waiting for a vacant berth. A week passed and Captain Stoker-Johnson, DSC, the master, was notified that a berth would be ready for him on Monday 4th January. This welcome news quickly spread through the ship and the crew, who had not set foot ashore since leaving Durban six weeks earlier, eagerly looked forward to some shore leave.

Sixty-two year old Oliver Stoker-Johnson had spent a lifetime in sail and steam and had been in command of ships for twenty years. In 1933 he had joined the Joseph Constantine Line of Middlesbrough as master of the *Brookwood*, and after two years had transferred to his present command. During his long years at sea he had narrowly avoided death on several occasions and over time had come to believe that a 'supreme being' was looking after him.

His closest brush with death came in 1916 whilst commanding the S.S. *Cyrene*. Whilst being attacked by an enemy submarine which had surfaced, he successfully escaped by keeping the ship's stern to the gunfire and during this action a shell passed through the bridge rails, just inches from his legs, before exploding on the foredeck. For his bravery under fire he was awarded the Distinguished Service Cross.

Ten years later in March 1926, Captain Stoker-Johnson was in command of the tramp steamer *Laleham*. Homeward-bound across the Atlantic, the ship was caught by a ferocious storm and began to founder and, with little hope of being saved, an SOS was sent out. This was answered by the steamer *Shirvan* of London, which battled mountainous seas to come to the rescue. Evening was rapidly drawing in and, with their lifeboats smashed, the crew of the *Laleham* knew that they would not survive the night. Volunteers from *Shirvan* courageously manned a lifeboat and, guided by blazing barrels of oil on the *Laleham*, they made two desperate forays to pluck all thirty-seven souls from the sinking ship. The eerie flickering of the flames in the darkness was the last that was seen of the *Laleham*, and her crew thanked their rescuers (all of whom received bravery awards) and God for their deliverance. After that experience, it became the custom for Mrs. Stoker-Johnson to hang a small silver horseshoe over her husband's cabin door. When he had assumed command of the *Kingswood* in April, his wife had come aboard and hung the lucky horseshoe with a sprig of heather over his door, and there it remained.

> 'So far as he was personally concerned, said the Captain, he was convinced that a guardian angel had watched over him in his career at sea'.
>
> *The Port Pirie Recorder,* 8th January 1937.

While at anchor on Sunday, 3rd January 1937 time was dragging as they waited to load. Captain Stoker-Johnson wondered what the New Year would bring as he finished breakfast and took his daily exercise walking up and down the bridge deck. Not far away below him in the engine-room, the second engineer and the donkeyman left to go and have their breakfast, having routinely increased the steam pressure of the auxiliary (donkey) boiler. Sunday was usually a day off for most of the crew when in port or at anchor, but this Sunday the engineers were busy raising steam on the main boilers in readiness for going alongside, a procedure that took twenty-four hours.

It was 8.30 am and already the fierce summer sun was beating down out of a steely blue sky. Captain Stoker-Johnson was determined to have his exercise before the oven-like heat of another Australian day inhibited any strenuous activity. Today it was the engineers who were busy, but tomorrow the deck department would be busy taking the ship alongside, opening up the hatches and positioning the derricks to work the cargo. He decided to go down to the main deck and take a stroll around. He was passing no. 3 hatch when suddenly a shattering roar split the silence of the morning and the captain found himself flung violently onto the deck. He was stunned for a few moments and, with blood running down his face, imagined he was badly injured. A black pall of greasy smoke enveloped everything and broken hatchboards and lumps of debris fell onto the foredeck.

Dazed and shaken, but with only a small cut on his forehead, Captain Stoker-Johnson had no idea what had happened. He guessed that there had been a terrible explosion in the engine-room and feared that men had been killed or maimed. Somebody helped him to his feet and he became aware of frightened shouts and men dashing past him. After the initial panic things quietened down and the crew gathered together on the boat deck. Word came that the engine-room was a compete shambles, but luckily no one had been on duty or they would have been killed. Apart from a few cuts and bruises, none of the crew was hurt and a roll call established that nobody was missing. Somebody shouted that there was something sticking out of the starboard bow and, fearing another explosion, the crew remained rooted to the spot. Captain Stoker-Johnson asked Jim Fryatt, his chief officer to investigate and Second Engineer Scott

Captain Stoker-Johnson had survived a number of life-threatening incidents during his long career, but the most unusual was a mysterious explosion on board the S.S. Kingswood. Photograph courtesy of the Australian Commonwealth Department of Transport & Regional Services.

went along with him. Summoning up courage, Chief Engineer Henry Davies led the rest of his engineers down into the engine-room.

It was as if the *Kingswood* had been torpedoed – there was no explanation as to what had happened. The ship was not taking water, but the two lifeboats were swung out as a precaution. There were few ships in the lonely anchorage and the sea was infested with sharks. It was a wise precaution because Chief Officer Fryatt and Second Engineer Scott breathlessly returned with the astounding news that there was a gaping hole in the starboard bow only a foot above the water line. They added that they were amazed the ship was still afloat and that wedged in the hole was the donkey boiler!

Everybody knew that the donkey boiler was bolted down in the engine-room so it was hard to believe it was now sticking out of the bow. Chief Engineer Davies was at a loss to explain what had happened. The engine-room and stokehold had been completely devastated and it appeared that an explosion had hurled the donkey boiler out of the engine-room. The main boilers had been unseated and the cylinders of the engine were grotesquely twisted out of line. The solid and dependable triple expansion engine was utterly wrecked.

A path of destruction told of the terrifying force of the explosion and the ship's officers cautiously climbed from the engine-room through a gaping hole that had been blasted through the steel bulkhead of no. 2 hold. They picked their way forwards where missing hatchboards allowed shafts of sunlight to penetrate the gloom. A stout wooden partition bulkhead had been smashed apart leaving sharp splinters spread out like porcupine quills as they inched their way through and across no. 1 hold. A jagged hole had been punched through the steel collision bulkhead and then they saw it – the boiler was embedded in the bow plating encircled by a broken halo of daylight. Although it had crashed against the steel framing the fearsome object was still intact. It was a chilling thought that if the donkey boiler had actually exploded it would have torn a huge hole in the hull, sinking the ship within minutes.

Slipping her anchor, the crippled *Kingswood* was towed into Port Pirie and nudged alongside the wharf under the gaze of several thousand spectators. The strange sight that the disabled steamer presented understandably attracted a great deal of attention. The fact that the ship had remained afloat and no lives had been lost was regarded as a miracle.

'I have no more idea than you what made that 15-ton boiler fly through 163 feet of the ship. The mystery may never be explained.

But by the intervention of a supreme power all hands on the ship are intact'.

Capt. Stoker-Johnson, quoted in the
Port Pirie Recorder, 8th January 1937.

Tied up alongside in Port Pirie, the black and green hull of the empty *Kingswood* rose up high over the wooden wharf. The boiler, protruding from a hole where the steel plates had been peeled back like banana skins, became the focus of investigation for expert boiler makers and marine engineers. The Joseph Constantine Line, the insurance underwriters and Lloyd's marine surveyors took a long time considering the best course of action. The ship needed to be dry-docked, her engine-room reconstructed and the trail of damage made good. It was unanimously agreed that the best place for this work to be done was at Newcastle-upon-Tyne where she had been built. Captain Stoker-Johnson was informed that a Dutch salvage tug was being sent from Rotterdam to tow the *Kingswood* halfway around the world to the Tyne.

Summer turned to autumn and local contractors prised the boiler free and patched the ugly hole in the starboard bow. The battered donkey boiler was stowed away to await a meticulous examination by its builders. A small auxiliary boiler was installed to turn the rudder, for without power to turn the rudders the ship would be impossible to tow for any distance. Languishing in Port Pirie some of the crew slipped away, some found berths on other British ships and others caused disturbances. Eventually only eight men remained to accompany the ship on her long tow home – Captain Stoker-Johnson, two deck officers, two engineers, the wireless operator, the cook and a steward. By April the ship was sufficiently seaworthy to face the rigours of a tow that, if successful, would be the longest ever tow of an ocean steamer by a single tug.

After three months of lying idle, the waterline of the *Kingswood* was thick with seaweed and barnacles and her paintwork had faded under the harsh sun. To the townspeople the ship had become a familiar sight, but when the Dutch tug *Ganges* appeared in the harbour things changed swiftly. Compared to the *Kingswood*, the tug looked deceptively small, but to the professional eye the massive power of her engines was unmistakeable. *Ganges* could pull a battleship if called upon to do so. She was skippered by Captain Klinge, who was the senior captain of the Smit organization's formidable fleet of ocean-going tugs. He was a big, jovial Dutchman who reassured everyone by declaring in excellent English that the forthcoming tow would be 'one of many, just one of many'. He would be in overall command of the tow and ten hands from his tug took up berths on the tramp ship to attend to the tow-line and to act as helmsmen.

Captain Klinge quickly began work. He was not in favour of having the *Kingswood* heavily ballasted, preferring to tow her 'light ship'. The blades of the propeller were removed to make towing easier and on board the tug an 18-inch towing hawser was heaved onto her afterdeck and coiled up. After a week of intense preparation, Captain Klinge was ready to put to sea. They would follow the regular steamer track from Australia to Europe via Suez, but since the *Kingswood* had plenty of coal in her bunkers the Dutch skipper boldly proposed making a short cut. Instead of calling at Colombo, they would stop at the remote Chagos Islands to refill the tug's bunkers from the towed vessel.

News of the tug's imminent departure spread through Port Pirie and on the morning of 27th April well-wishers lined the wharves to wave farewell. They were rewarded with the thrilling sight of the squat, powerful *Ganges*, black smoke pouring from her tall funnel and with the sound of her siren reverberating across the harbour, towing her disabled charge out to sea. It was the beginning of a remarkable 15,000-mile voyage that would make maritime history.

Chapter 21

Sailing Without Orders

The Hain Steamship Company operated a large fleet of ships and had many years of experience in the tramping trades. The black funnel with its bold white capital 'H' made the ships easy to identify, although the port of registry in white across the stern, St Ives, must have puzzled many a foreign dockside worker. They would not know that St. Ives was a small Cornish fishing village where the company was founded, although the fleet was actually based at Cardiff.

Charles Cordy was born in Cardiff in 1890 and joined the Hain Line as an apprentice. He passed his master's certificate at the end of the First World War and was given his first command, the S.S. *Trehawke*, in 1922. The Hain Company moved him from ship to ship and when he took command of the S.S. *Tregenna* at the end of 1929, it was his seventh command in seven years. In April 1930 *Tregenna* was at Barry loading best steaming coal for Santos, Brazil's coffee port. It seemed logical that she might lift a cargo of coffee but, being a tramp ship, nothing was certain. It was just another voyage for Captain Cordy, who knew the ports of Brazil and Argentina like the back of his hand. After eighteen days at Santos, it came as no surprise when orders were received to sail in ballast to Kingston, Jamaica for bunkers and thence to two Cuban ports, Casilda and Santiago de Cuba, to load sugar.

In 1930 the small Cuban port of Casilda consisted of a roadstead between a barrier of reefs and the coast. The *Tregenna* lay anchored 2 miles offshore, her derricks busily lifting slings of heavy sacks of sugar from lighters nestled alongside. The ship was empty and riding high in the water, making loading a slow process and, with the ship ready to slip anchor in the event of bad weather, no shore leave was allowed. Captain Cordy could not leave the ship either and had to rely on the ship's agent coming out to the anchorage with his sailing orders. Everyone was relieved when the time came for the *Tregenna* to up anchor and sail for the sheltered harbour of Santiago de Cuba.

The harbour of Santiago de Cuba lay some 350 miles further eastward along the coast and had been built by the Spanish over 400 years before. Its narrow entrance was guarded by the imposing Morro Castle, behind which stood a lighthouse painted a dazzling white. Both the castle and the lighthouse were visible from several miles out at sea, although the entrance channel itself was difficult to distinguish because of the high cliffs that towered over it. Choppy seas and deep water made anchorage anywhere outside the harbour entrance inadvisable.

Once at the sugar-loading berth, Captain Cordy learnt that the *Tregenna* had been chartered by the Tate & Lyle Company and was to deliver 7,700 tons of sugar to their refinery at Greenock. Santiago de Cuba was a bustling port with a railway, sugar mills, tobacco warehouses, cigar factories and a famous rum distillery and consequently harbour berths were at a premium. After only

A mislaid cablegram resulted in the Treganna *deviating from her charter.* Photograph courtesy of the State Library of South Australia.

four days the loading of sugar ceased. Captain Cordy was at a loss to understand why, for the vessel only had 5,000 tons in her holds. With the rainy season coming on the port authorities urged him to clear the berth, insisting that there was no more sugar consigned to the *Tregenna*. With thousands more tons of sugar to export before the rains and other ships due to arrive, Captain Cordy would have to move his ship.

With no orders to sail, in fact with no orders at all, Captain Cordy was in a dilemma. He was short of 2,700 tons of sugar, and the local ship's agent could not offer any explanation or advice. Anchoring in the unsafe waters outside the harbour to await orders was out of the question, so he decided to sail for Greenock. As far as he was concerned the charterers had chosen not to load a full cargo and would pay dead freight (when cargo space is paid for but not actually loaded). The *Tregenna* duly sailed, but just thirteen hours into her homeward voyage the wireless operator handed Captain Cordy a most urgent message. The *Tregenna* was to proceed immediately to the Dominican Republic port of San Pedro de Macoris where she was to load 2,700 tons of sugar.

San Pedro de Macoris lies on the southern coast of the Dominican Republic, the port being about half a mile from the sea on the east bank of the Rio Macoris. The town was a centre of commercial activity and consisted of numerous wharves, sugar mills, factories and many fine villas. The entrance of the River Macoris was known to be treacherous due to the shifting shoals that extended seaward. It was usual for ships with deep draughts to load partly in the port and then move out to the designated anchorage to complete loading. On arrival the *Tregenna* was directed to the anchorage and on the morning of 2nd August her anchor was let go in 5 fathoms of water, about 600 yards offshore. Since Captain Cordy had not been to the port before he was concerned that the ship had anchored too close to the entrance channel. However, the agent's clerk, who had come out in the Custom's launch, assured him that it was quite usual. By anchoring close in, the lighters would not have so far to come and loading of the sugar would take a few days, rather than a few weeks. The clerk did not know why Captain Cordy had not received any sailing orders at the previous port.

Despite the heat and humidity, Captain Cordy donned his best white uniform and promptly took the launch ashore to find out what had been going on. Hurrying through his obligatory visit to the British Vice Consul to deposit the ship's articles, he wasted no time in calling into the agent's office where, over a long cool drink, the events of the past few weeks were explained to him. Unknown to Captain Cordy, the charterers had telegraphed the all-important sailing orders to him at Casilda where, unfortunately, the telegraph line stopped short some 5 miles from the town. The solution was to pay someone to deliver any incoming telegrams to Casilda and, in this instance, a passing truck driver had been entrusted with the sailing orders. The orders directed Captain Cordy to proceed to a third port, San Pedro de Macoris, to complete the loading. For some reason the truck driver had not delivered the telegram to the agents so when the *Tregenna* arrived at Santiago de Cuba no one was any the wiser. It was assumed that Captain Cordy had received his orders and would carry on to San Pedro de Macoris as instructed.

In the world of tramp shipping, contracts made between ship owners and charterers are known as charter parties. The charter party is a standard document which clearly sets out the details of the voyage to be made, and unless it was for the purpose of saving life or property, a ship was not expected to deviate from an agreed voyage. Any unjustified deviation was regarded as a serious matter and could lead to protracted legal claims and in this case, by missing out the third loading port, the *Tregenna* had, for whatever reason, deviated from the contracted voyage. Upon leaving Cuba the direct route for San Pedro de Macoris was southward, but the ship had gone northward and this had added an extra 260 miles to the voyage. Captain Cordy was blameless but he understood that the Hain Shipping Company was liable to be held responsible for the costs involved in the deviation.

Back on board, the captain busied himself with the practical business of getting the ship loaded. Swinging at anchor and lifting cargo from lighters was a busy time for the deck officers and besides attending to the loading of the cargo, they were constantly taking bearings of the tall chimneys of the sugar mills to check if the ship was dragging her anchor.

Undercurrents of insurgency and revolution were sweeping through the Dominican Republic at that time, but it was business as usual at San Pedro de Macoris. The holds were soon full with the tough stevedores forcing the heavy and bulky sacks into a locking pattern to secure them. Five days later on 7th August the hatches were closed, the locking bars put into place and the derricks lowered. Charles Cordy even found time to relax in his cabin with a pure Havana cigar – visiting Cuban ports did have its compensations. The windlass finally clanked the anchor home and with the engine building up to full revolutions, this time the *Tregenna* was genuinely homeward-bound.

On the bridge the engine-room telegraph handle was pushed down to full ahead and the ship's bow was swinging around to head out to sea, when the wheelhouse began to shiver alarmingly. Instead of gathering momentum and making for the open sea, the ship appeared to be going nowhere. The engine was stopped and, from the discoloured sea water surrounding the vessel, it was obvious that they were over a sandy shoal. The engine was alternately put astern and ahead without any noticeable effect – the *Tregenna* obstinately refused to budge. Captain Cordy could hardly believe that the ship had gone aground just outside the harbour entrance. He ordered both anchors to be dropped to steady the vessel. In view of the forthcoming hurricane season it was imperative that the ship was moved from her exposed position and the only course of action was to start offloading the cargo until she floated free. Sugar was an expensive commodity and it would be necessary to transport thousands of sacks ashore to lighten the ship by even a few inches. Any idea of dumping them straight over the side was rejected.

Discharging into lighters was going to be an expensive and time-consuming operation. No. 2 hold, the largest of the five holds and which contained 2,000 tons of sugar, was found to be leaking badly. The sugar greedily absorbed the water, adding extra weight to the vessel's displacement, and all of the sacks contaminated by sea water were heaved over the side. Having only just cleared the ship to sail with the port authorities and the British Vice Consul, Captain Cordy now had to present the ship's papers again for 'arrival' and the articles were duly stamped 'Vessel arrived 9th Aug. 1930'. The days passed and as work ceased every evening the lights of San Pedro de Macoris twinkled invitingly from the nearby shore. It was the calm before the storm because the dreaded hurricane season was only a few weeks away.

Everything was being done to save the *Tregenna*. American divers from the salvage steamer *Warbler* assessed the damaged to the hull as being confined to the starboard side, extending from the bow to the after bulkhead of no. 2 hold. Twenty frames were bent and many bottom plates and rivets had sprung leaks. By keeping the ship's bilge pumps operating continually and by emptying the holds of all cargo, it seemed that the ship would be saved. The only unpredictable factor was the weather.

Eventually by 22nd August the ship could be felt bobbing on the tide and with the sugar discharged and temporary repairs made, she was able to sail under her own steam to Newport News, Virginia, to be dry-docked. It was a narrow escape because on 3rd September a violent hurricane swept across Santo Domingo and whipped up tremendous seas along the southern coast.

The *Tregenna* had barely escaped one storm when she and the Hain Shipping Company ran headlong into another, different type of storm, and one that would take six years to ride out. Who was legally responsible for the considerable losses and expenses incurred by the ship's owners, the charterers and the owners of the sugar cargo? Who was ultimately responsible for deviating from the voyage as laid down in the charter party? It took the lawyers a long time to apportion the blame but Captain Cordy found another captain waiting to take his place as soon as the *Tregenna* was safely in dry dock. The endorsement in the ship's articles made by the British Vice Consul at Newport News on 30th September 1930 leaves little to the imagination.

> 'I hereby certify that Capt. C. Cordy has this day been superseded by Capt. Richard Harvey, whose certificate of competency is no. S.S. 008411.
>
> British Vice Consul at Newport News,
Ship's Articles, 30th September 1930.

Chapter 22

A Heroic Second Mate

T he London-based company of Watts, Watts & Co. Limited was well-known in the shipping world. During the late 1920s the fleet consisted of over thirty ships, most of which were second-hand and elderly tramp steamers. Exceptions were the *Watford, Wanstead* and *Wendover* built in 1928 for the company at the Caledon Yard in Dundee. These sister ships were specifically designed to carry bulk cargoes for long distances, the type of trade in which Watts, Watts & Co. specialized.

The *Watford* could carry 9,000 tons in her five holds, the hatches of which were slightly larger than usual in order to facilitate loading and discharging. The vessel could carry a crew of forty with eight seamen whose quarters were on the port side of the fo'c's'le, the bosun and carpenter having their cabins on the starboard side. The deck officers, chief steward and wireless officer each had a cabin on the bridge deck and separated from the bridge deck by no. 2A hold was the boatdeck, where the engineers' cabins occupied the port side. The starboard side had shared cabins for four apprentices, two cooks and two stewards. The firemen were berthed under the poop and in exceptionally bad weather could access the engine-room through the shaft tunnel. Her accommodation was an improvement on the standard design where the crews' quarters were under the fo'c's'le head. With her teak wheelhouse and bridge, the ship was one of the smartest and most modern of her day, and was only four years old in 1932.

In April of that year the *Watford* was under charter to the Dominion Steel & Coal Corporation (known as DOSCO)of Sydney, Nova Scotia. The ship was required to load at DOSCO's piers in Sydney Harbour at the eastern end of Cape Breton Island, Nova Scotia, and shuttle industrial coals to Montreal during the ice-free season. They were short, repetitive voyages with not much time for shore leave. Navigation through the Gulf of St Lawrence was particularly demanding because, as well as the constant proximity of land, the area was busy with shipping. River traffic was heavier than ever that year as exports of Canadian grain had reached record levels.

On 7th September, once again leaving Montreal in ballast for the four-day return leg to Sydney, her master Captain Penrud contemplated whether the ship would keep trading until December when the lower St Lawrence would begin to freeze over. With her holds completely empty and bunker coal at less than half, the *Watford* was riding high so that in the placid waters of the harbour the tips of her four-bladed propeller were breaking the surface. After several months of plying the St Lawrence, Captain Penrud and his officers had accumulated a good working knowledge of the 500-mile river and had no reason to suppose that this trip would differ from any other. They expected to be back under DOSCO's coal tips late on Saturday, 10th September as scheduled.

By the Friday evening, steering a south-easterly course through Cabot Strait, a gale began to brew and strong winds built up from the north-east. Pushed by cross currents it became impossible to hold course. Plunging on during the night through raging seas and driving rain, Captain Penrud pushed on towards the shelter of Sydney Harbour which lay approximately 100 miles ahead, experience telling him that the gale would probably peak around midnight.

By midnight the winds were gusting at 100 miles an hour, a velocity of hurricane strength which had never been previously recorded along the coast of Cape Breton. Surfing the mountainous seas, the *Watford* was being tossed about like an empty box and Chief Engineer Cook warned Captain Penrud that with the screw constantly out of the water, the racing of the engine and the violent vibrations of the propeller shaft would result in serious damage. In an effort to sink the rudder and propeller into the water, Captain Penrud ordered the fore peak tanks to be pumped dry and with the after peak tank already being full, he ordered no. 5 lower hold to be flooded. This had some effect at last and, as an indistinct dawn was breaking, the light on Flat Point which marked the approach into Sydney Harbour was sighted. Captain Penrud, Chief Officer William Knight and Second Officer Herbert Mant, who had all spent the night in the wheelhouse, breathed a sigh of relief. The captain's unusual method of saving the ship had worked, and it was only a matter of rounding Flat Point and they would be in sheltered water.

Relief quickly turned to despair when the dawn distinctly revealed the outline of the shore. The situation had become precarious as the ship was slowly but surely being blown backwards and, worse still, shorewards. Flat Point beckoned tantalizingly, but there was no hope of reaching it. Captain Penrud had many years of seafaring under his belt and knew that the *Watford* and her crew were in dire straits.

Following Captain Penrud's instructions, Wireless Officer Charles O'Donnell was already in touch with North Sydney Radio and reported that the *Watford* was in trouble. For several stomach-churning hours, the ship was driven back along the coast. The east coast of Cape Breton Island was rocky and desolate and for several hours the crew watched apprehensively through a curtain of rain as the coast came nearer and nearer. Captain Penrud gauged that the ship had been blown 20 miles southward and was somewhere off Cape Percy. He doubted if the *Watford* would clear that precipitous headland and saw to it that life-jackets were issued to the crew. The wireless operator sent a final message, just before the main aerial was blown away.

'In very dangerous position, no. 2 hold flooding'.

The ship's foghorn forlornly called for help as blurred glimpses of the rugged coast became more infrequent. These were quickly lost, obliterated by driving rain and sheets of spray. A nightmarish hour passed with the crew resolutely remaining at their posts until the very last moment. With heavy seas breaking over her, the *Watford* slammed against the rocks and, caught by the unrelenting hurricane force winds, bumped and crashed her way to within 300 feet of a low cliff. Slewing around so that her starboard side was parallel with the cliff face, the ship stayed on an even keel, her hull split and punctured by huge lumps of granite.

Plans for abandoning ship were put into action and Chief Officer Knight and the bosun, a no-nonsense Shetlander named Donald Murray, organized the swinging out of the starboard lifeboat. The ship's bottom had been ripped to shreds and the hull began to split amidships as they worked. Fearing that the vessel would break up before they could get off, Captain Penrud gave the order to abandon ship. The crew clambered into the lifeboat but, realizing that it had no chance in the furious cauldron of water below, Captain Penrud ordered the men out again. Conditions were so bad that one of the firemen who had gone into the lifeboat straight from stoking the furnaces, was found to have died from exposure.

A safer way of getting the crew off the ship was by using the hand-held rocket gun to fire a light line ashore, but since there was no sign of life on the bleak cliffs, it meant that there was no-one to seize such a line and make it secure. A call went round for a volunteer to swim ashore to make fast the lifeline. The *Watford* was

405 feet long and the swimmer would have to swim almost that distance through the dreadful sea to reach shore. It would take a brave man to attempt it but on hearing Captain Penrud's appeal, Second Officer Herbert Mant promptly volunteered. Taking off his warm uniform and tying a light line around his waist, he plunged into the sea. He was rapidly swept towards the shore but when he disappeared under the surging foam it was feared that the line was hindering him, and it was released. After struggling for some time, Herbert Mant had the good fortune to find himself in shallow water. Although thoroughly chilled and exhausted, he managed to scramble up the rocky cliff.

The timely arrival of some local men, bent double against the appalling winds, and who had followed the ship along the clifftops, was a godsend for Herbert Mant. After being given some warm clothes he was able to instruct them how to rig up a lifeline. Two rocket lines fired from the ship were borne by the wind and deftly landed close to the waiting group of men. The lines were securely tied to one of the few stunted trees that grew on the clifftop. Meanwhile, several troopers from the Royal Canadian Mounted Police led a rescue party to the scene. Stronger ropes from the *Watford* were sent ashore and a bosun's chair (a wooden seat used when working aloft) was attached to a pulley so that it could be pulled ashore and then back to the ship. The first man fairly flew ashore when pulled by the rescuers. The boatdeck of the *Watford* was slightly higher than the cliffs and hauling the empty bosun's chair back against the wind was difficult and needed a great deal of strength. It was taking about five minutes to haul a man the 300 feet to shore and another ten minutes to pull the bosun's chair back against the tremendous wind. Working non-stop, the rescue proceeded smoothly until by late afternoon only Captain Penrud, Chief Officer Knight and the bosun, Donald Murray, were left on board.

Fatigued by the continual blast of wind and soaked by spray, Captain Penrud declared that he would be the last to leave, although he was not physically strong enough to haul the bosun's chair back on board by himself. There was a delay as the three men argued the point, but eventually Captain Penrud was persuaded to take his place in the chair and, still protesting, was whisked ashore. A similar impasse then arose between the chief officer and the bosun. Reluctantly agreeing that the bosun was the one who had sufficient strength to haul back the chair on his own, Chief Officer Knight wearily climbed into the chair. Seeming to lose his concentration, he somehow slipped, fell into the boiling sea and was swept away. It happened so quickly that Donald Murray could do nothing but instinctively grab the empty chair. He then carefully climbed into it himself and was hauled ashore.

Frozen and wet, the crew had been sheltering in the nearby solitary house and later that evening were taken to Sydney where they spent the remainder of the wild and stormy night in the Navy League House. Two of their number had died but the rest were saved due to the unstinting help of the Cape Breton Islanders.

Back in England, the gallantry of Second Officer Herbert Mant did not go unnoticed. On 12th October he was presented with a fine telescope from the Officers' (Merchant Navy) Federation in London, and on 1st November he attended Lloyd's in London where he was awarded the Lloyd's Silver Medal for Saving Life at Sea.

A month later he received a silver medal and a diploma from the Royal Humane Society, and the culmination of these awards came on 20th December when King George V presented him with the Board of Trade Sea Gallantry Medal at Buckingham Palace.

> 'The King, on the recommendation of the President of the Board of Trade, has awarded the Silver Medal for Gallantry In Saving Life at Sea to Herbert Mant, Second Officer in the S.S. *Watford*, of London.'
>
> *The Times*, 21st December 1932.

While serving as Second Mate, Herbert Mant displayed grat courage when the S.S.Watford was wrecked. Four years later he was master of the Farnham which was bombed and sunk at Alicante in 1938. Later in 1940 his ship was bombed and destroyed at Rouen. Whilst in command of the Ashcroft a few months later the ship was posted missing, presumably torpedoed west of Ireland. Photograph courtesy of the National Maritime Museum, London.

Chapter 23

Mutiny on the S.S. *Luciston*

The S.S. *Luciston*, affectionately known as the 'Lucy' was owned by W.S. Miller & Co. of Glasgow. Their half a dozen ships were invariably to be found tramping in the less attractive trades and their drab paintwork and all-black smokestacks reflected the spartan existence of those who sailed in them. One of the company's charters was with the British Phosphate Company carrying phosphate rock from the Pacific islands of Ocean and Nauru. The rock was in great demand by Australian wheat farmers as fertilizer and a host of tramps was needed to satisfy the demand.

Captain Malcolm Macdonald was born in Inverness in 1882 and although he was aged forty-six, he looked much older. The long years of sailing on Glaswegian tramp ships had taken their toll and he was not a well man. Ill feelings from the previous voyage between himself and the chief officer and the chief engineer still rankled, and he was not looking forward to spending another long voyage with these two resentful officers.

Arriving at Newcastle, New South Wales in November 1928, the ship went on time charter to the British Phosphate Commission. The dismal prospect of this monotonous charter to and from the islands did not appeal to everyone and the cook deserted. At such short notice a qualified replacement could not be found and the steward, Charles Lobeck, who was an ex-cook, was persuaded to return to the galley, thus allowing the ship to sail on time. There was no anchorage at either Ocean or Nauru Islands and ships often spent endless days waiting for perfect weather before it was safe to go in and tie up at the mooring buoys. Proof of the dangerous nature of the elements was that two ships – the S.S. *Ooma* and the S.S. *Ocean Transport* – had only recently been swept ashore and wrecked at Ocean Island. After a week of drifting off Ocean Island and with no foreseeable break in the weather, the *Luciston* was sent to Nauru Island, a distance of 180 miles, to load her first phosphate cargo of the season.

Secured to the loading buoy at Nauru, the tramp steamer became a hive of activity. The derricks were raised and the hatches thrown open as the winches strained at heaving up the heavy baskets of grey rock from the lighters ranged alongside. As the baskets were tipped into the four gaping holds, clouds of choking dust rose up and coated the ship. By counting the number of baskets loaded the tonnage could be estimated, but with the vessel rolling uneasily in the Pacific swell it was difficult to read the mean draught. A ship's master had to be careful in this respect for the Australian authorities would fine any ship that entered port overloaded. With 7,000 tons of rock in her holds the *Luciston* was cleared to sail for Geelong, near Melbourne.

Christmas Day 1928 was spent on the Australian coast with Charles Lobeck being the busiest man on board as he sweated in the galley to produce the traditional Christmas dinner. He did his best but his cooking did not please everybody, particularly the twelve Africans who shovelled coal in the stokehold. They complained bitterly that they wanted a proper cook and when the ship docked in Geelong they barricaded Charles Lobeck in the galley as a protest. However, the unenviable vacant berth as a ship's cook on a run-down tramp failed to attract any applicants, and after a speedy discharge the *Luciston* was sent back to Nauru.

Off Nauru and drifting on a glassy sea, time was hanging heavily. There were several other steamers ahead of them and the *Luciston* would have to wait her turn to load. Just before dawn, Chief Engineer Hugh Purdie called upon Captain Macdonald for help. One of the firemen had gone berserk but Captain Macdonald apprehensively edged down the steep engine-room ladders and managed to calm the man. He noted the incident in the log book.

> 'W. Cole, fireman, at 4 am this date refused to obey orders of the chief engineer in respect of his duties, for disobedience to lawful command first offence I log and fine him five shillings, and record this entry as tantamount to mutiny by the above man.'
>
> Official log book, S.S. *Luciston*, 11th February 1929.

As he wrote the entry it did not occur to him that this might be a precursor of things to come. Loaded and with Nauru barely out of sight, troubles in the engine-room took a different turn. Second Engineer Thomas Turnbull became ill. Aged fifty he was a veteran and his practical knowledge of steam engines was probably greater than that of Chief Engineer Purdie. Told that the second engineer had collapsed, Captain Macdonald entered the port alleyway that ran alongside the engine-room and entered Thomas Turnbull's cabin. The din and vibration were terrific but that was something that all ships' engineers took for granted. Thomas Turnbull was past caring, he lay doubled up in his bunk with severe stomach pains and a temperature of 102°. Captain Macdonald prescribed two spoonfuls of castor oil, ten drops of morphine and eleven drops of essence of peppermint – and hoped for the best.

Consulting his medical handbook, Captain Macdonald decided that his patient was suffering from enteric fever or perhaps an inflammation of the bowel. At this point the British Phosphate Company ordered *Luciston* to deliver her cargo to Fremantle rather than Geelong, which would add another ten days to the voyage. The second engineer could not wait that long for treatment so Captain Macdonald obtained permission to put into the nearest port, Port Kembla, thus saving Thomas Turnbull's life.

A typical tramp ship, the S. S. Luciston was run on a shoestring and carried low value cargoes that gave little profit. Spending long weeks in the Pacific waiting to load made the ship a hot bed of intrigue and insubordination. Photograph courtesy of the National Library of South Africa.

Apart from three of the firemen delaying the ship by trying to desert, all went well at Fremantle and the *Luciston* was once again sent back to Nauru. Loaded, and with Geelong as her port of discharge, Captain Macdonald looked forward to a trouble-free voyage. This was not to be as he then became unwell with severe toothache. With considerable misgivings he handed over command to Matthew Anderson, his devious and ambitious chief officer.

Chief Officer Anderson took over command with great enthusiasm but, to his chagrin, the ship remained tied up at the discharge berth and on the very eve of sailing Captain Macdonald, who had been ashore to have all his teeth extracted, unexpectedly resumed command. A brief stop at Port Kembla to pick up a fully-recovered Thomas Turnbull, and the *Luciston* was on her way to collect another load of phosphate at Nauru. To everyone's relief, this time the ship was called straight in to the mooring buoy. From his vantage point in the wheelhouse, Captain Macdonald could see that loading was going well despite a strong swell. A double ring on the ship's bell reminded him that it was one o'clock and time for lunch. He turned to go when he was confronted by the white-overalled figure of Hugh Purdie. The chief engineer blurted out that the firemen were flatly refusing to work, and he was therefore unable to keep steam up which posed a serious threat to the ship. The weather was always a risk at Nauru, and ships had to be constantly ready to slip the mooring and sail out to sea. The firemen had some grievances that could not be readily settled, and when the ringleader, a tall, muscular African named Alfred Penfunran, shouted abuse at him, Captain Macdonald sent a message ashore for help.

A tense night passed before the island's police launch was seen approaching and, rather self-consciously, two uniformed policemen came up the accommodation ladder. Penfunran and his cronies took refuge in their quarters under the fo'c's'le head and refused to come out. It was left to Captain Macdonald to instruct the policemen to arrest Penfunran. However, faced with such aggression, the policemen retreated to their launch and hurried ashore to report, leaving Captain Macdonald and his officers to solve the standoff.

There the matter rested until the Administrator of Nauru requested a meeting ashore with the captain. Although not happy about leaving the ship, Captain Macdonald had little choice and found himself sitting uncomfortably in the Administrator's office. The Administrator outlined the situation. He could, of course, issue a warrant for the arrest of Penfunran and the others but had the captain considered the implications? There could be violence, the ship could be delayed by further problems with the crew and the ship's owners and charterers would not be pleased. In his judgement it would be more prudent to avoid further trouble and get the ship out to sea.

Twenty-four hours later, the *Luciston* was fully loaded and heading out to sea. The firemen were cock-a-hoop with their victory, insubordination was rife and threats to kill the cook unless his cooking improved were made. With this uneasy atmosphere on board, the ship received orders to take her cargo to Fremantle.

Somewhere off the south Australian coast the breakdown of discipline in the engine-room finally came to a head. Despite repeated attempts, Chief Engineer Purdie had been unable to get the firemen to do the essential maintenance of periodically scaling the boilers and when the centre boiler began to show tell-tale signs of neglect, it was closed down immediately. With one boiler down the ship needed to go to Port Adelaide for repairs. Once berthed, all three boilers were examined by a Lloyd's surveyor. The centre boiler was found to have been burnt by a build-up of excessive scale and the port and starboard boilers were in poor condition and needed cleaning. He also discovered that the centre boiler was cracked. The state of the boilers reflected poorly on Chief Engineer Purdie and it was estimated that repairs and cleaning would take a month. The *Luciston* was taken off charter and her phosphate cargo discharged whilst shore labour was employed to put the boilers into working order.

With a patch welded over the crack in the centre boiler *Luciston* went back on charter and was sent to Ocean Island. She arrived on 2nd December 1929, almost a year since she had been there last. Day after day of tropical heat and inactivity passed as the ship drifted offshore waiting to be called in to load. Tempers became frayed and even Henry Longthorn, the normally imperturbable carpenter, complained bitterly about the food. (The crew's grievances were later upheld on returning to the United Kingdom, when they were paid £1.10s each for short provisions.)

Three weeks dragged by before Chief Engineer Purdie decided to close down the port boiler for cleaning. The very next day the ship was called into the mooring. Not obeying the signal to commence loading would be breaking the terms of the charter, yet the mooring at Ocean Island was dangerous even with full steam on all boilers, as the wrecks of the *Ooma* and *Ocean Transport* testified. The concise engine-room standing orders did not convey Captain Macdonald's worry.

> 'Engineers and firemen on anchor watches, full head of steam to be kept up and the engines heated up ready to proceed at very short notice.'

Christmas and Boxing Day were spent on the mooring. They were cheerless affairs with poor food and Hogmanay promised nothing better. On Boxing Day night, unwell and irritated by some of the officers playing cards outside his cabin, Captain Macdonald shouted at them to go away and leave him in peace. Chief Officer Anderson, in particular, took offence to this and spread a rumour that Captain Macdonald was drunk. A few hours later when the wind began to freshen, the captain decided to clear the mooring and head out to sea and safety.

Warning the engineers that full steam was needed, the mooring was slipped and the telegraph put to full ahead. To Captain Macdonald's consternation, the engines failed to respond and before he knew it the wind and sea had pushed the *Luciston* towards the dark reefs and the menacing hulk of the wrecked *Ooma*. The ship bounced hard against the bow of the wreck just as the engine burst into life and the *Luciston* made headway. The episode had not been without cost. In attempting to raise steam rapidly on the cold port boiler, a process that normally took twenty-four hours, Chief Engineer Purdie had filled it with sea water and had steam up in only five hours. This was a desperate measure because fresh water was the life blood of a ship's boilers and using sea water would cause great damage.

Twenty more days of interminable waiting for a break in the quirky weather passed before the ship was able to return to the mooring to complete her cargo. At 9 am on 16th January the sea was deceptively calm and the hatches were open ready to start loading. Twenty-five minutes later everything changed. A terrific rain squall appeared at hurricane force and heeled the empty ship over. The mooring cable snapped and the *Luciston* was catapulted stern first towards the fringing reefs. On the bridge, Captain Macdonald threw the engines to full ahead and this time they responded instantly. The propeller bit into the coral reef and the rudder post took a hefty blow, but the ship kept on going and once again *Luciston* reached the safety of the open sea.

With her stern post and rudder damaged and all the propeller blades missing their tips the ship was indeed lucky to be afloat. Any further loading was out of the question and a message was relayed to W.S. Miller & Co. in Glasgow. Meanwhile the stern post was strengthened with chains and wire lashings, and Captain Macdonald received a cablegram from the owners to proceed immediately to Japan for repairs.

In the opinion of the ship's officers, the steamer was not sufficiently seaworthy to reach Japan and they favoured Brisbane. After a night of furtive discussion, Chief Officer Anderson handed Captain Macdonald a letter of protest.

S.S. *Luciston*

At sea

9.10 am, 22nd January 1930.

Captain Macdonald

Dear Sir,

We, the undersigned officers and engineers refuse to proceed further than the nearest port where repairs can be executed. We do not consider the steamer sufficiently seaworthy to proceed any further.

Every assistance will be given to you to accomplish getting the steamer to the nearest port without assistance.

Signed:
M. Anderson — Chief Officer
H. Purdie — Chief Engineer
T.G. Young — 2nd Officer
F.T.G. Perrin — 3rd Officer
Thos. Turnbull — 2nd Engineer
Archd. Taylor — 3rd Engineer

With not a single officer supporting him, Captain Macdonald was completely alone. Visions of being imprisoned by his officers flashed before him and, after hesitating for a moment, he backed away from any confrontation. Mutiny was a serious business and he did not want to ignite it. He swallowed hard and said, "Very well, Mr Anderson, the protest is noted. We shall proceed to Brisbane."

In Glasgow the owners of the *Luciston* were displeased. It made good economic sense for repairs to be carried out in a Japanese port and then quickly get the vessel back on charter. Arrival at an Australian port might suit the ship's officers, but for a company running on a tight budget, red tape and expensive labour were to be avoided at all costs. Their fears were proved correct. From Brisbane the *Luciston* was sent to Sydney to be dry-docked, therefore losing her charter and consequently losing money. Captain Macdonald was summoned to a Court of Marine Inquiry at Sydney on 24th and 25th February 1930, on a charge of being drunk whilst in charge of the *Luciston*. The allegation had been made to the Australian authorities by Chief Officer Anderson and Chief Engineer Purdie. Their motives were mischievous and were subsequently discredited during the inquiry. The court found unanimously that the charge against Captain Macdonald had not been sustained. It had been a harrowing time for him and his sickly appearance was commented upon during the two-day hearing.

After weeks in dry dock, the *Luciston* lay at anchor in one of Sydney's quiet coves while her owners were endeavouring to find a cargo of wheat to bring her home. One day a launch brought out two men dressed in civilian clothes. One scrutinized the ship with seasoned eyes while the other was far more interested in the engine-room. They had come from Scotland travelling as passengers on a P&O liner and they were W.S. Miller & Co's marine superintendent and senior master who had come to take charge of the *Luciston*.

Chapter 24

Admiralty Chart 1001

October 1936 found the S.S. *Bury Hill* nearing completion of loading a full cargo of wheat worth the enormous sum of £65,000 at Bunbury, Western Australia. Her master, Captain Walter Smith, was anxiously waiting for a cable from the ship's owners in London giving him his sailing orders. At the age of thirty-five the young Welshman had been in command of the *Bury Hill* for exactly two years and three months. He had taken the ageing tramp to the usual destinations of South Africa, Canada, South America and Australia but at Bunbury, dockside rumour had it that the cargo of wheat was consigned to a Chinese port.

It was not practical for a company to supply a tramp with every conceivable chart, and upon being sent to some faraway port, it was up to the master to obtain the appropriate charts. The chart locker of the *Bury Hill* had no charts of China and Captain Smith could not find any to purchase in Bunbury. However, when his orders arrived they instructed him to sail for the United Kingdom via Durban and Dakar.

Captain Smith knew Durban very well, but was not familiar with Dakar. Unfortunately, a check of the locker showed that there was no chart of the approaches to Dakar Harbour, and if his recent visit to the Bunbury chandlers was anything to go by, he despaired of finding one quickly. With the ship ready to sail, he assured himself that he could easily find any chart he wanted in Durban. On 20th October the ship sailed, and although recently overhauled by her owners, the Sussex Steamship Company, she was over nineteen years old so it was a slow but steady crossing of the Indian Ocean. Thirty-one days later the powerful beam of Durban's lighthouse high on the Bluff was picked up 40 miles out by the officers of the *Bury Hill* and in the early dawn of Friday, 13th

November the tramp slowly passed through the entrance channel into Port Natal. A berth was allocated on the mile-long quay known as the Point and bunkering began immediately. Durban served as a bunkering port for many British ships on the long haul between the United Kingdom and Australia, and for a ship to arrive and leave on the same day was not unusual.

Soon a series of bangs and crashes reverberated from the cross bunker hatch as tons of coal were dumped into the bowels of the ship. Captain Smith took his briefcase and set off to complete his round of official calls. Even entering harbour for a day involved the signing of numerous documents. The Point was the busiest section of the harbour and the offices and shops of a multitude of shipping agencies, provedores (Chinese merchants who provided supplies to ships) and chandlers were clustered around it. As expected, Captain Smith's orders from the owners were that he leave that day for Dakar. He called in the nearest chart agents, fully expecting to obtain a copy of Admiralty chart no. 1001 – *Africa West Coast, showing Dakar and its Approaches.* To his annoyance it was not in stock. There was only one other chart agent in Durban, so Captain Smith had to extend his sojourn ashore and go there. Again, it was not in stock, although every other chart imaginable seemed to be available. Frustrated, Walter Smith returned to his ship. Rummaging around in the chartroom he found a tracing of part of chart 1001 which showed some of Dakar Harbour and which must have been used previously. Incomplete as it was, it would have to suffice.

The *Bury Hill* put to sea again that afternoon and began an unhurried three-week voyage to Dakar. Apart from the western approaches to the English Channel, the sea lanes around the south-east coast of South Africa were the busiest in the world, with scores of tramps and liners continually rounding the Cape of Good Hope. Until Cape Town was well astern, Captain Smith gave up sleeping in his cabin and stayed on the bridge, taking a rest now and then on the chartroom settee. A sharp lookout was essential in South African waters, especially at night, as some ships continued to use oil-burning navigation lights which did not shine too brightly. Captain Smith had no experience of West African ports since they were well-served by cargo liners on fixed schedules. Tramps seldom called unless, homeward-bound, they called into Dakar for bunkers, and in this case, the *Bury Hill* was so heavily loaded that she had not been able to take on enough coal at Durban to complete her voyage.

Captain Smith had taken command of the *Bury Hill* in July 1934, when the ship's enterprising managers, the Kulukundis Brothers of Bury Court in London, had purchased the veteran ship on their own account. After reconditioning and renaming her, they readily obtained charters that sent the ship carrying grain to and from a wide variety of ports. Although the ship was old, having been built in 1917, she was strong and her mahogany wheelhouse and bridge, newly-painted funnel of yellow with white and blue bands and red star, gave the ship a good-looking appearance. The *Bury Hill* was fully equipped in every respect and was in a good and seaworthy condition.

The approach to Dakar from the south is by the Baie de Goree, one of the most beautiful maritime approaches in Africa. Golden beaches backed by verdant jungle extend as far as the eye can see, and from seaward the city dominates the western shore. Dakar was the capital of French West Africa and standing out from the sprawling township were the Catholic Cathedral and the minaret of the grand mosque. Fronting the fine, deep water harbour is the Isle of Goree, and when the French harbour pilot boarded the *Bury Hill* he enlightened the ship's officers as to its grim history. He pointed out the forbidding castle where countless slaves had perished whilst waiting to be shipped across the Atlantic. However, Captain Smith paid scant attention for he was hoping to see a friendly British steamer in harbour where he could be certain of getting some advice and see an up-to-date chart. He knew that leaving Dakar was not straightforward as it meant rounding the rugged Cap Vert peninsula before heading out into the Atlantic.

It was popularly believed by many mariners that Cap Vert itself marked the western extremity of Africa, but it is actually Almadi Point, two miles to the north, that has this distinction. It also has a notorious jumble of reefs that extend a further mile out to sea. In 1936 the remains of no less than four merchantmen were visible stranded on this reef, and even Admiralty chart 1001 (1976 edition) shows five wrecks impaled on Almadi Reef. Captain Smith's inadequate tracing of chart 1001 did not include Almadi Point, and one glance at the proper large scale chart would have shown him the position of the light tower high on that point which warned mariners to keep well clear.

Dakar Harbour is formed by two breakwaters 720 yards apart. Invariably French merchant and naval vessels were present along with the odd British, Greek or Italian steamer. Unfortunately for Captain Smith there were no Red Ensigns to be seen. Shortly after midday on Saturday 5th December the *Bury Hill* passed sedately between the harbour breakwaters to go alongside. The day was hot and the surface of the harbour was like glass as the pilot turned the steamer without the use of tugs and placed her with her bows facing the entrance. At 3 o'clock on the sweltering afternoon no orders had yet arrived, so Captain Smith authorized shore leave for the crew. He notified the owners in London that the ship had arrived safely and hopefully requested the local ship's chandler to provide him with Admiralty chart 1001. Ships usually had the necessary charts before they entered port, so it was no surprise to find that one of the approaches to Dakar was not in stock.

The next day, Sunday, was a free day for those of the crew who could arrange to leave the ship. In contrast to English-speaking Durban, it was a surprise to the crew to realize that every African spoke perfect French and finding their way around the city was not easy. Monday morning saw the port come alive with commercial activity and it wasn't until after lunch that Captain Smith was handed a cable to proceed to Falmouth for orders, a stock phrase which meant that the charterers were still undecided about the best port to land their cargo. It was seventeen days to Christmas and the buzz among the crew was that they would be spending New Year's Eve somewhere on the Continent.

It was compulsory to leave harbour with a pilot and accordingly Captain Smith booked one and obtained harbour clearance for 9 o'clock that night. The harbour lights were shining dimly in the warm darkness and the sea was as smooth as a millpond when the tramp left her berth and slipped out through the breakwaters. She moved into the fairway between Pointe de Dakar and Goree Island, the pilot was dropped off and the engine-room telegraph rung at full ahead. The ship slowly built up to her maximum speed of 8 knots whilst Captain Smith conned the *Bury Hill* seawards guided by the flashing red channel lights. Third Mate Walter was officer of the watch and together the two men stood on the bridge wing continually sweeping the night with their binoculars. The lights of Dakar were well astern, but ahead on the starboard bow the reassuring beam of the Cap Vert light was flashing and slightly further ahead there appeared the faint stern light of a ship. Captain Smith and Third Officer Walter recalled that a steamer had sailed an hour or so before them and decided that she was the vessel ahead. They spent twenty minutes observing this apparently stationary stern light, Captain Smith using his telescope for a better look. He could definitely make out the shadowy superstructure of a steamer which was on his starboard bow and he was convinced that the white stern light belonged to this vessel. Confident in his assessment, he handed over the ship to the third officer and left the bridge. It was six bells or 11 pm.

Alone on the bridge, Third Mate Thomas Walter had an hour of his watch to go. It had been a tense time carefully conning the ship away from Dakar, but he could afford to relax a little as the ocean swell began to make the vessel rise and dip. At 11.40 he distinctly heard the sound of breakers ahead and, instantly alert, he believed that the helmsman had wandered off course. At the same moment flashes of white phosphorescence caught his attention. There was no

The S.S. Bury Hill. *The veteran tramp ship was seventeen years old when the Sussex Steamship Co. bought her 'as she lay' for £8,500. After spending a further £4,500 on reconditioning, the vessel was renamed and classed A.1. at Lloyds. The* Bury Hill *was then employed on worldwide tramping for several years until she stranded on a reef in December 1936.*

time to call the master so Thomas Walter rang the engine-room telegraph to full astern. A swift glance at the compass showed that the helmsman was steering the given course, so he shouted at the startled seaman to get the wheel hard over. It was no use and with a horrendous scraping the entire 400-feet length of the *Bury Hill* crashed against the Almadi Reef.

Within the minute Captain Smith was on the bridge and with the exception of those in the engine-room, the crew lined the starboard rail and peered into the menacing dark waters that surged over the reef. The engine was stopped and the familiar rhythmic thumping of the triple expansion machinery was replaced by an unsettling clanking as the pistons idled. A long, ear-splitting screech screamed into the night as excessive steam was blown off by the engineers. Unsure of where his ship was and what had actually happened, Captain Smith ordered the port lifeboat to be swung out and the bilge pumps engaged. It was soon realized that the ship was stuck fast and was probably badly holed. The pumps were coping well and, as a precaution against being pushed further onto the reef, the port anchor was let go. After informing Dakar of the ship's plight, there was little else that could be done until morning.

With the sunrise many brightly-coloured fishing canoes crammed with Africans clustered around the ship. The natives had come to regard wrecked ships as manna from heaven and they reaped quite a bounty from the wrecks on the reef. Their most recent haul had been from the Norwegian tramp steamer *Beryl*, whose gaunt superstructure was now revealed. It was this wreck that had deceived Captain Smith, for directly behind it was a tall cylindrical tower, on top of which was Almadi Point Light. The mystery of the stationary stern light was solved. The range and characteristics of Almadi Point Light were clearly shown on Admiralty chart 1001, but not on Captain Smith's inferior tracing. Somehow the wreck had partly obscured the beam, creating an illusion of a ship's stern light.

Twenty of the crew were taken into Dakar by the French authorities, leaving eleven men who volunteered to stay on board. The presence of four wrecks close by did not bode well for a successful salvage, and the restless ocean swell constantly sweeping over the reef made the hull creak and groan. Nevertheless, Captain Smith persevered and hoped for the best. The old, strongly-riveted hull stood up to some heavy pounding for twelve days before the inevitable happened and the Kulukundis Brothers in London received the news they had been expecting. 'Broken amidships, advise Dakar to discharge crew'.

It was all over, the *Bury Hill* had broken her back and was a total loss. The old ship was left to the French scrap merchants and the dugout canoe entrepreneurs to dismantle and pick over.

Chapter 25

Making Legal History

The red-tiled houses of Whitby line the steep banks of the River Esk and cluster around the harbour. Whitby is one of the most beautiful towns on the north-east coast of England and is well-known for the romantic ruins of its ancient Abbey and for its association with Captain Cook. The *Endeavour, Resolution, Discovery* and *Adventure* are Whitby's most famous ships, but the S.S. *Crusader*, owned by the Eskside Steam Shipping Co. of Whitby, also has a claim to fame. This obscure tramp steamer sailed into British legal history when the misadventures of her master in the Indian Ocean resulted in a legal dispute being decided in the High Court.

In June 1903 Captain Fred Brown, aged fifty-five, a Welshman from Penarth, was exceedingly glad to find himself in command of the S.S. *Crusader*. The ship was only two years old, her accommodation was first rate and she was a large and most useful steamer for the carriage of bulk cargoes. She was the pride and joy of the small shipping company which was prepared to pay well to have an experienced and dependable master look after its interests during the ship's long voyages, which could be anywhere in the world.

Captain Brown was welcomed on board by a group of officers who were very much younger than himself. Chief Engineer Geoff Johnson was thirty-one and Second Engineer Parkinson was twenty-two, both men being from Ryhope near Sunderland. Chief Officer George Clarkson and Second Officer John Milburn were just two years older, and both from Whitby, while Third Officer Charles Crossley was only twenty. Captain Brown was by far the most experienced officer and it was his sole responsibility to navigate between ports, negotiate with what were perceived to be grasping ships' agents and maintain discipline on board.

about 2 miles ahead when the *Crusader* unexpectedly bumped and bucked and, cursing loudly, Captain Brown abruptly stopped the engines. The ship grated to a standstill as she had struck a reef. Needing no orders, the crew apprehensively congregated on the boatdeck clutching their life-jackets and some favoured possessions. Captain Brown had no intention of abandoning ship and told the crew so in no uncertain terms, using a megaphone. Tensions eased when sounding of the bilges showed that the ship was leaking but in no danger of sinking. Soundings around the ship showed that there was only 3 fathoms of water forward where she had become embedded in the coral, but over 200 fathoms under the stern.

Trying to see if the ship could be eased off into deep water, the engines were cautiously run astern. This had no effect and Captain Brown decided to wait until daybreak to jettison cargo from the forward holds to lighten her before trying again. Sleep was impossible; there was the clonk, clonk of the donkey pump, the unpredictable shriek of steam being let off, and under the crew's quarters in the fo'c's'le head the eerie sound of steel grinding on rock was unmistakeable.

At first light the derricks on the foredeck were topped and no. 1 hold was opened up. The sea was placid and as each heavy bale of sugar was lifted out and dumped overboard hopes were high of getting the steamer off. It was a daunting task to empty the two forward holds of their cargo, but if the men worked with a will there was every chance that the *Crusader* would be refloated. Captain Brown stressed the urgency of the situation, since his plan would work only if the weather held and even promised the men a bonus. He was somewhat taken aback by the attitude of the 'black gang' (firemen were inevitably covered in coal grime, hence the name) who believed that their duty was to stoke the furnaces, but no more than that.

Sights taken at noon established that the *Crusader* was 12 miles south of Kardiva Island, and was aground a mile north of Gopar Island. The two islands were similar in appearance and, in the darkness, Captain Brown had mistaken one for the other. With a high tide due late in the day, work on dumping the cargo ceased. All effort was put into using the ship's two lifeboats to carry the port anchor with a wire rope attached as far astern as possible. It was dropped and at the right time the windlass began to heave on this as the engines were run astern, but to no avail, the ship refused to move.

The crew returned to the work of dumping the sugar in the intense heat. It was difficult not to admire the scenery, for the sea was a deep blue and there was a strong smell of the tropical islands that lay about them. Tantalizingly close was a small island with golden sands and coconut trees, but as they laboured under the glaring sun their energy began to drain away. The next day another attempt to kedge the vessel free ended with the loss of the anchor when the wire rope snapped, but the ship had moved. Still held forward, a strong current had slowly swung her round until the starboard side was hard up against the reef. By this time, many inquisitive natives had come out to the ship in an assortment of craft and intimated that their sultan would be pleased to offer assistance. Captain Brown seized this opportunity and wished to hire many men to speed up jettisoning the cargo.

Shipwrecks were not uncommon in the Maldives, the most recent being the S.S. *Umona* in 1903, and the narrow escape of the S.S. *Nithsdale* the year before. The Maldivians had previously been suspicious of Europeans, but gradually realized they could expect to be well paid for helping steamships in trouble. The captain realized that this was an opportunity to send a message for assistance to Colombo. If he could summon the tug *Goliath* to come to his aid, then the *Crusader* could be pulled off the reef.

It appeared that the sultan's palace was close by and the correct thing to do in the circumstances was for Captain Brown to pay his respects. However, he was in no position to leave the ship so he delegated the honour to young Chief Officer Milburn. Apart from negotiating the price for the native labourers, John Milburn endeavoured to persuade the Sultan to send a message quickly to Colombo. Officers of tramp ships were not noted for their fondness of uniforms, but wearing the best one that could be found, Chief Officer Milburn set off to meet the Sultan of the Maldives. Two anxious nights passed before a large buggalow with two masts and lateen sails of coconut matting came up to the *Crusader*. The figure of John Milburn clad in his white uniform stood out clearly amongst the near naked brown bodies of the native crew. He was in high spirts as he clambered on board, announcing that all was well. The natives would work for silver rupees, and a buggalow had been placed at Captain Brown's disposal to take a message to Colombo. John Milburn was enjoying his adventure and when Captain Brown asked him to go with the buggalow and personally deliver a letter to the ship's agents, he enthusiastically agreed.

S.S. *Crusader*
Maldives

11th August 1905

Messrs Clarke, Young & Co.
Colombo

Dear Sirs,

    This will introduce you to Mr Milburn, Chief Mate of the *Crusader*. Kindly give him every assistance and draw disbursements on my owners. The *Crusader* ran ashore here the night of the 7th instant. I am jettisoning cargo forward, but as the reef is so steep, having under the stern of the steamer over 200 fathoms of water, and forward only 16 feet, I can make no use of the anchors, having lost already stream anchor and new wire rope. The Sultan of the Maldive Islands has kindly promised me assistance as to labour, but that alone will not get the steamer off as the current sets on the reef, and as we lighten so we drive further on. A salvage boat would be of assistance on the principle of 'no cure, no pay'. I will probably be able to make better terms here than you can at Colombo with salvage boat when he sees the situation. So far she is only leaking slightly in fore peak and no. 1 tank. Please inform Lloyd's agents. My Chief Officer has telegram and letter for my owners, which please forward. Despatch of tug is of the utmost importance, so do not delay.
    I am, dear sirs,

Yours faithfully
Fred. Brown,
Master, S.S. *Crusader*

P.S. Please send me Rs 500* by Chief Mate to pay labourers for lightening and pumping at fore peak.
(*A silver rupee was worth 1s 4d [7p] and a fireman on the Crusader was paid £1 per week).

Within the hour the buggalow was sailing for Colombo, the native crew assuring Captain Brown that his message would be delivered in four days' time. It would therefore be over a week before the tug could be expected, by which time the vessel would be several thousand tons of sugar lighter. Although not taking on water, the *Crusader* had begun to list to port, causing Captain Brown some concern. The Maldivians swarmed on board and cheerfully worked down in the oven-like holds attaching slings to the bales of sugar. The derricks worked non-stop at lifting and dumping the cargo overboard and with perfect weather day after day, the prospects of getting the ship off the reef seemed good. Captain Brown even began to consider whether to take the ship back to Colombo or go directly to Bombay for dry docking.

However, on 17th August, seven days since the departure of the buggalow, Chief Engineer Johnson reported that the plates of the engine-room floor were buckling. By lightening the forward holds of over 2,000 tons of cargo, and with the stern floating in deep water, the ship was sagging in the middle. This was extremely serious as further lightening could break the back of the steamer. After ten days of struggle all work was stopped and the fate of the *Crusader* hung in the balance.

Early the next morning the welcome sight of a tug ploughing towards them raised the spirits of everyone on board, although Captain Brown doubted if the ship could now be pulled free. Towing her off the reef would most likely rip the bottom plating open, and the weakened hull would crack. However he was reluctant simply to abandon the steamer where she lay. The tug came closer and by her salt-caked appearance it was obvious that she had been driven hard. All hands lined the rails of the tramp and cheered loudly as the tug came alongside. Chief Officer Milburn was the first to board and, awkwardly clutching the satchel full of silver rupees, he was roundly welcomed by his fellow officers. Following him was Mr. Young, representing Clarke, Young & Co., and Captain Rankine, the tug skipper. After the pleasantries were over, a heated discussion took place in Captain Brown's cabin.

With the best interests of his owners at heart, Captain Brown was adamant that the salvage of the *Crusader* would be on a 'no cure, no pay' basis. He had already decided that the reward for refloating the ship was to be £4,000. He alone was well aware that even if the ship was pulled free, she could still sink, in which case there would be no pay. However, the agents, Messrs Clark, Young & Co., had not been able to secure the services of *Goliath* on a 'no cure, no pay' contract, and instead had hired her for fourteen days at £60 a day. This agreement had been approved by cable from the ship's owners in Whitby. Captain Brown openly expressed his mistrust of any deals made without his knowledge and simply refused to accept it. With negotiations at a standstill, Captain Brown declared that if his original terms were not accepted then the tug could return to Colombo.

Faced with an intransigent Captain Brown, Mr. Young was unsure of the consequences if the steamer was left to her fate. Alternatively, his firm would earn a handsome profit if the *Crusader* was refloated and towed back to Colombo. It was a gamble, and he dubiously decided to allow the tug to go ahead, but first he was obliged to sign a document that Captain Brown thrust upon him.

'This is to certify that I as master of this ship and on behalf of my owners, the Eskside Steam Shipping Co., Whitby, have this day agreed with you to pay Messrs Clarke, Young & Co. (on the 'no cure, no pay' system) the sum of £4,000 if you succeed in floating the *Crusader* and see her safely into the nearest port if required. In the event of your doing so a payment to be made by draft on my owners. It is of course understood that should you not succeed in floating the steamer I am to pay you nothing'.

By noon the *Goliath* had made fast to the stern of the *Crusader*, but refloating the ship was put on hold until the next morning's high tide. At 7 am, the tug took up the strain and the engines of the tramp were put astern, but nothing happened. Captain Rankine was not going to risk wrenching the ship free, but suggested further lightening of the holds until the high tide peaked in the afternoon. At 2.30 pm another attempt was made, and with great excitement the stern of the tramp was pulled clear, but the midships section remained stuck. Captain Rankine experimented at pulling the stern from various angles. At 3.50 pm the tow rope broke, but Captain Rankine knew the ship was within inches of breaking free. Impatiently he ordered a new tow rope to be made fast, and with great expertise he persuaded the tramp out of her rocky berth. By 5 pm the *Crusader* was free and floating in deep water. It had been a long, hot day's work and Captain Rankine was rightly congratulated for a job well done. Contrary to expectation, the *Crusader* was not seriously damaged and was able to make Colombo under her own steam.

Once the ship was in harbour, Captain Brown's first priority was to take action against the trouble-makers on board his ship.

'Mutinous Behaviour of the Crew

During the time the ship was stuck on the reef some of the crew gave Captain Brown considerable trouble by refusing to obey orders. Captain Fred. Brown of the Crusader brought four European sailors (belonging to the above vessel) to the Joint Police Court late this afternoon to charge them with refusing to work'.

The Ceylon Observer, 23rd August 1905.

These men were put in jail for a month and others were signed on in their places. With no dry dock at Colombo, the rest of the sugar was discharged and the vessel sailed to Bombay for repairs. Captain Brown became aware that the Eskside Steamship Co. was none too pleased with him over the way he had disregarded their agreement with Clarke, Young & Co. The ship's agents were now claiming £4,000 for having succeeded in floating the Crusader whereas, under the original agreement, the bill would have been less than £1,000. Not surprisingly, the owners of the tramp ship had declined to recognize Captain Brown's 'no cure, no pay' document and wished to settle for the lesser figure.

To add to Captain Brown's worries he was required to surrender his master's certificate to the District Court of Colombo and face an enquiry into the grounding of his ship. Cross-examination on Saturday, 2nd September revealed that the chart he had used was too small a scale and inadequate for accurately plotting the ship's position. To pass through the unlit Five Degree Channel at night was unwise, especially if the ship's position was not accurately known, and for these reasons Captain Brown was censured for imprudence. The fact that he had not been absent from the bridge and that cloudy conditions had made celestial observations impossible permitted the court to return his master's certificate to him.

After spending a month at Bombay, the *Crusader* returned to Colombo to reload the saved proportion of her cargo, which was still worth £30,000 – almost equal to the value of the ship. Prudently passing through the Five Degree Channel in daylight, Captain Brown took her through Suez and finally to Liverpool where he had little option but to resign his command.

Clarke, Young & Co. went on to sue the Eskside Steamship Co. for £4,000 and, when the decision went against them in the High Court, they appealed. The appeal was dismissed for two important reasons. Firstly, a ship's master had very wide powers of acting on behalf of his owners but if, in certain circumstances, his actions could be assessed as unreasonable, then his owners need not be bound by such actions. Captain Brown was found to have acted unreasonably in demanding his 'no cure, no pay' agreement.

Secondly, it was also established that a ship's agent could not act in a manner that was adverse to the best interests of a ship owner. Their interests were therefore identical and in this case Clarke, Young & Co. were precluded from seeking a salvage award, but were entitled to all expenses and agency fees.

Who could imagine that the stranding of the *Crusader*, the actions of Captain Brown and the adventures of Chief Officer Milburn would be preserved in the Law Reports of 1906/1907, and that such an exciting tale of the sea would be found on the shelves of a university law library!

Chapter 26

The Confusing Harbour Lights

Glancing at Admiralty chart No. 1920 of Table Bay, South Africa, one notices a small symbol denoting a wreck 'showing a portion of hull or superstructure' off the sandy dunes of the Cape Town suburb of Milnerton. How a ship came to be wrecked within sight of the Table Bay docks is a story of one misfortune after another.

It was July 1934 and the South Australian wheat port of Thevenard was busy with ketches and railway wagons bringing heavy sacks of golden wheat up to three tramp ships. The *King Arthur*, the *Fife* and the *Winton* were using their own derricks to each load around 90,000 sacks of wheat bound for Britain. The *Winton* was the last of the three to sail and sitting deep in the water from the weight of 7,000 tons of wheat, she began the long voyage home. The ship belonged to the Avenue Shipping Company of London and usually traded to Australia via the Pacific but this was the first time she would be going around the Cape of Good Hope for the homeward voyage. Being a motor ship, her only port of call would be Cape Town to take on heavy fuel oil and her master, Captain Christopher Mordaunt, was interested to see the 'Tavern of the Seas' again as he had not called there for many years.

Christopher Mordaunt had had a long career. A Somerset man, he had been a shipmaster for twenty years. He had joined the small Avenue Shipping Company in 1925, taking command of their M.V. *Enton* on her maiden voyage. Three years later the company acquired a brand new motor vessel, the *Winton*, and Captain Mordaunt was given her command. With the subsequent loss of the *Enton* in 1931 on a reef off New Caledonia, responsibility fell upon Captain Mordaunt to ensure that the seagoing side of the small company business ran smoothly.

Trusting the wrong red light, the Winton's *captain went past the anchorage and on to the sandy Milnerton Beach at Cape Town.* Photograph courtesy of the Edwardes Collection, State Library of South Australia.

After a voyage of three weeks, the *Winton* raised the Cape of Good Hope on a wintry Saturday 28th July. The ship steered northwards and followed the rugged Cape's peninsular coastline until shortly before 8 pm when the Green Point Lighthouse was abeam. With Table Bay just ahead, the signalling station next to the lighthouse flashed a message that the *Winton* was to anchor where convenient for the night. The expense of a night docking was to be avoided and the ship would probably lie at anchor until Monday morning to save port dues.

It was a miserable night and a drizzling rain had the effect of softening the glare of the lights of Cape Town. Standing on into the waters of Table Bay, visibility was poor and, with no other ships at anchor, there was not even the gleam of a single anchor light to guide the *Winton* in. Captain Mordaunt put the engine at half ahead to continue across the bay. Against the city lights he needed to make out the flashing red light on the harbour breakwater in order to verify his position, but decided it must be very dim because it was not visible. He was disturbed by Third Mate Walter Stevens as he came into the wheelhouse to relieve William Buckingham, the first mate. Eight bells sounded as the watches changed and the first mate put on his thick serge coat to keep out the cold and left the bridge to go forward to take charge of letting go the anchor.

Intent on giving the rocks of Green Point a wide berth, Captain Mordaunt kept the carpet of hazy lights that covered the base of Table Mountain well to starboard. The sea was smooth with little swell and there was complete darkness all around. On the fo'c's'le head the brake on the windlass was eased, walking the starboard anchor out so that it was hanging clear of the hawsepipe ready to let go. On the bridge Captain Mordaunt and Third Mate Stevens studied every likely light along the shoreline searching for the elusive flashing red light that marked the harbour breakwater. Finally spotting it, Captain Mordaunt altered course keeping the light very close to the direction the ship was steering. After a while he stopped the engine and gradually allowed the ship to lose way before anchoring. Captain Mordaunt judged that he was about 2 miles from the breakwater light and he gave the order to let go the anchor.

On the fo'c's'le head the carpenter stood ready to release the windlass brake and send the anchor plunging into the dark water below. First Mate Buckingham had never been to Cape Town but he had heard that coming into the bay could be difficult in the dark. The ship was slowing down and he expected to hear the command to let go the anchor at any moment. Unexpectedly, the bow of the ship began to tremble as if somehow the anchor chain was paying itself out. Apprehensively, he leant far out over the bow rail to see if the anchor was still hanging from the hawsepipe. It was and he realized that the *Winton* had run aground!

On the bridge, Captain Mordaunt was keeping an eye on the flashing red light. There were no other harbour lights that he could make out and, as far as he was concerned, the black void ahead was the open water of Table Bay. He told the third mate to let the engine-room know they would be anchoring and that the engines were to be kept ready during the night in case a gale should blow up.

To anchor in an open roadstead was a straightforward manoeuvre. With the engine stopped and the ship losing speed, the anchor would be let go, then the engine put slowly astern and when plenty of cable had been laid out the engine would be stopped. It was a routine that all ships' officers knew very well. Captain Mordaunt turned and glanced at the clock, it was 9.15 pm, he was just about to order the anchor to be let go when he glimpsed a dark line directly ahead. Frowning, he swiftly rang full astern.

Down below the engineers were expecting the ship to anchor and reacted promptly, slamming the engine into reverse. The ship shivered as the screw bit deeply in an attempt to pull the ship free from the clinging sand that threatened to entrap her. The *Winton* vibrated furiously as Captain Mordaunt held the handle of the engine-room telegraph firmly at full astern. He willed the ship to break free but it was no use. Angry with himself for being in this situation, he moved the handle to stop and went out onto the starboard bridge wing to study the surface of the dark water below, but the green glow of the sidelight revealed nothing. He ordered the helm to be put hard over to starboard, and with the engine at slow ahead he rammed the handle back to full astern in an effort to work the ship free. It made no difference, the *Winton* remained stuck fast.

Without further ado, Captain Mordaunt put out a call for help. He was confident that a modern port like Cape Town would send a tug out almost immediately and tow him free. Waiting anxiously, he had time to assess what had happened. To his astonishment he found that he had mistaken a red flashing light on a radio mast for the red flashing breakwater light. The characteristics of these red lights were similar, but a few miles apart. Somehow, against the panorama of the city lights, he had confused the two. Pacing the bridge, Captain Mordaunt became increasingly agitated. The tide was on the ebb and it was past midnight before a tug belatedly came out to him. The harbour tugs were not on constant standby and it took time to assemble their crews and get steam up. By early morning two tugs were in attendance, and Captain England, the port captain, had taken charge of the operation to free the *Winton*. He explained that only recently a red light had been placed on top of one of several tall wireless masts at Milnerton as a warning to aircraft. There was little doubt that this red light was a hazard to mariners and indeed the S.S. *Indian Prince* had briefly run aground only three months previously because of this.

In the grey hours of early dawn, towing wires were passed across and both tugs stood ready to start heaving. With high tide peaking at 8 am the rescue began. It was a dull overcast morning and the solid mass of Table Mountain provided a sombre backdrop to the drama taking place off Milnerton Beach. The propeller of the *Winton* was driven forcefully in reverse whilst the tugs strained at the stern, and hopes were high as the ship began to move. Another few minutes and she would have been dragged free from the clinging sand. Then came disaster. One of the tight towing cables snapped and, as the tug shot forward, the long flailing end of the wire whipped backwards and became entangled in the *Winton*'s propeller. With fathoms of 2-inch wire enmeshed around the propeller, the main engine of the *Winton* was effectively jammed and the rescue attempt ground to an unwelcome halt.

By now, South African radio had broadcast the plight of the *Winton* and thousands of people made their way to Milnerton Beach to view the proceedings. Although it was winter, the beach achieved an unheard of popularity and families were even picnicking on the sands. One newspaper commented that 'wreck watching had become one of Cape Town's major pastimes', and the struggle to refloat the ship filled the newspapers for days to come.

Working from a lifeboat, Chief Engineer Miller took charge of a party that hacked away at the tightly-packed wire which was strangling the propeller. There was no quick way to lighten the ship because the tightly-stowed sacks of wheat could only be unloaded, or dumped, by working methodically. Nevertheless, lighters and gangs of labourers were brought alongside to start taking off the cargo. On the evening high tide the tugs tried to drag the ship free but without the use of her propeller the *Winton* predictably refused to budge. Her hull had become embedded in the soft sand, and Captain England was no longer cheerfully predicting that the ship would be off on the next high tide.

Local knowledge was that the present calm sea was due to change and, as Sunday wore on, strong winds and the notorious westerly swells of Table Bay began to hamper the rescue operation. The stern of the ship started to bump on the sandy bottom and, being so heavily loaded, the rudder post and tail shaft took a battering. By Monday evening the weather had deteriorated so much that it was decided to take the thirty-four crew off the *Winton*. They clambered down the ship's side by means of a rope ladder onto the harbour tug, the *Ludwig Weiner*. One of the last to leave was Albert, the ship's parrot, who angrily squawked in protest.

A break in the weather the next day promised a reprieve for the freighter. The crew hurriedly returned and Captain England was anxious to make one last all-out attempt to free the ship. Nobody wanted to admit it, as the tugs had already strained their engines to the limit and, indeed, broken more tow ropes than any other salvage operation in Table Bay, but it was doubtful if they would succeed now. However, it was just possible that the swells had rocked the ship free of the deadly sands but, on the other hand, they could have worked the ship deeper into a sandy grave. Captain England wanted to use the harbour dredger to scoop out an escape channel for the *Winton*, but, as luck would have it, it was in dry dock. They nevertheless had to try but, as had been feared, the ship did not move and remained embedded in the sand. The crew abandoned their ship for the second time and the sea quickly took its toll, waves remorselessly pounding the hull until it cracked amidships. That night a fire broke out and in the morning the *Winton*, fire-blackened and with her back broken, had become a completely unsalvable wreck.

It was felt by the seasoned skippers who regularly called at Cape Town that the recently-displayed red light at Milnerton was ill-placed. There was strong support for this view and, during the two weeks spent waiting for the Court of Inquiry to be held into the loss of his ship, Captain Mordaunt became a respected figure amongst the marine fraternity of the Cape. He had already decided that whatever the outcome of the Court of Inquiry he would be leaving the sea. As each day passed he could not avoid looking out over Table Bay and, seeing the battered wreck of the *Winton*, he wondered how such a thing could have happened. It was some consolation when the Court of Inquiry duly found that the stranding of the vessel was due to Captain Mordaunt confusing the Milnerton Light with the Breakwater light, but since he could not be criticized for that he was therefore absolved of all blame.

It was puzzling that although the Milnerton Light had certainly misled other ships' masters, the question remained why the Government had been slow to remove it. Although Table Bay was a safe and well-equipped harbour, Captain Mordaunt felt embittered that his ship had been wrecked within its confines. He was convinced that

'The ship could have been saved if a tug had arrived immediately he signalled for assistance.'

Court of Inquiry, Cape Town, 15th August 1934.

Three years later, the Supreme Court of South Africa overturned the findings of the Court of Inquiry and found that the stranding of the *Winton* was due to

'... the grossly negligent manner in which she was navigated'.

The wreck of the *Winton* was well away from the approaches to Table Bay docks but her rusting superstructure and the recurring symbol of the wreck on subsequent editions of Admiralty chart No. 1920 served to warn mariners to be doubly cautious before putting their trust in the harbour lights.